D1488795

While waiting at the 8/24/07
airport in Kalamazoo I
came across this book.
I enjoyed reading it on
my way to Florida.
    Hope you can relate to
the trees, birds, etc in
Michigan.

                    Lois Krull
                    2007

OF WOODS AND OTHER THINGS

Henderson

EMMA BICKHAM PITCHER

OF WOODS AND OTHER THINGS

BEECH LEAF PRESS
KALAMAZOO, MICHIGAN

Copyright © 1996
Beech Leaf Press
Kalamazoo, Michigan
All rights reserved. No part of this publication may be repro-
duced or transmitted in any form or by any means, electronic or
mechanical, including photocopy, recording, or any information
storage and retrieval system without permission in writing from
the publisher.
Library of Congress Catalog Card Number: 95-083950
ISBN 0-939293-18-4
Printed in The United States of America

For
Rachel Carson
Margaret Nice
Mary Oliver
and
Ann Zwinger

For
Hal Borland
John Madson
John McPhee
and
Eliot Porter

They have illumined my life.

Contents

Introduction

Nature writing of necessity involves two delightful occupations: roaming around wild places observing flora and fauna and later poring over relevant books attempting to learn more. In such pleasant ways do naturalists grope toward understanding. Questions always remain—leading to the next foray. Fortunately, the learning never ends.

Nature writers are linked to the earth in a particularly satisfying way because careful observation requires slowing down to note structure, texture, arrangement of feathers or leaves. A serendipitous discovery brings such joy. We are drawn to these life-giving rhythms of nature. In *The Biophilia Hypothesis*, Harvard University biologist Edward O. Wilson calls this feeling biophilia, "the innately emotional affiliation of human beings to other living organisms."

The Kalamazoo Nature Center has long been known for its educational efforts on behalf of the natural world. Since 1986 it has contributed a weekly interpretive column to the Kalamazoo *Gazette*. Authors may be staff or community volunteers. Of the 130 essays I have contributed since 1988, about half are included in this work. Such writing is an author's dream: no assigned topics and no deadlines.

The collection was edited to freshen the essays and eliminate repetition.

Acknowledgements

I offer my very warmest thanks to each and every person who has been part of my adventure in nature. Forty years of woods watching means that many people have shared ideas and insights.

I give special thanks to Monica Ann Evans of the Kalamazoo Nature Center to whom I am deeply indebted. She has helped me both cheerfully and efficiently from the day of my arrival in Michigan. Her knowledge, experience, and editorial skills shaped the book in many ways, especially when she was the contact person with the Kalamazoo *Gazette*. Monica capably captained the editorial team of Valerie Noble, co-editor, Elizabeth Henderson, artist, and Ann Paulson, designer of this book. To all, I express my gratitude.

I am most thankful to past and present staff members of the Nature Center who have made me welcome: Raymond Adams, Patricia Adams, Stephen Allen, Leonard Chase, David Evers, Constance Ferguson, Jean Gal, Sarah Hopkins, Richard and Brenda Keith, Gail McPeek, Sarah Reding, and Willard Rose.

It is a pleasure to acknowledge the help of various academicians whose words and writings have been important to me: Norbert Blei, Richard Brewer, Kenneth Brock, Elwood Ehrle, Richard Pippen, Floyd Swink, Steven Tonsor, Edward Voss, Gerould Wilhelm, and Dennis Woodland.

I express deep appreciation for the gracious friendliness of Lois and James Richmond and the wonders of their Nature's Acres where I spend many pleasant days in peaceful observation and study.

I offer my heartfelt thanks for the vote of confidence expressed by those whose generous financial support helped make the book a reality: Anonymous, Margaret Dooley, Monica Ann Evans, James Hammond, Charles and Marguerite Hoffman, Edwin and Mary Meader, Valerie Noble, Barbara Plampin, James and Lois Richmond, and the Shirley Heinze Environmental Fund.

We appreciate the Kalamazoo *Gazette's* years of cooperation in publishing the weekly "Nature's Way" columns, its contribution to local environmental education.

Finally, I will never forget the many friends and students who have been my mentors in woodland hours spent together: Delano Arvin, Lee Casebere, Kenneth Dritz, Sonja and Conrad Fischer, Ilse Gebhard and Russ Schipper, James Hammond, Edith Harris, Ronald Heibert, Irene Herlocker-Meyer, Myrna Nugent, Noel Pavlovic, Barbara Plampin, Douglas Rood, Bobbie Squires, Robert Tweit, and Blair Winter, among a host of others.

Henderson

Of Feathers

I Love Birds

Birds! I love birds! I love their joie de vivre, their jauntiness, their gaily colored feathers, their pure whistles and rollicking songs, their unique adaptations to habitats and food supplies, their superb maneuvering skills, their amazing migratory flights.

What's the lure? What joys keep me entranced after forty years of watching? What discoveries still capture my imagination? Why is it still such fun to find a bird I've never seen before? What are the memories? There are so many.

In the joie de vivre category I enjoy: the deliberate picking and choosing process a white-breasted nuthatch goes through as he selects the perfect sunflower seed from among sixteen others he has already tested; a flight of snow geese or sandhill cranes high, high, high in the blue, mere specks, but their myriad calls drift down symbolizing nature's abundance; a long-tailed jaeger in the Arctic flying with such fluid grace as to seem weightless; statuesque long-billed curlews gracefully swinging their heads from side to side, moving like ballerinas. Can they be real?

And remembering their feathers I recall: a red-legged black-necked stilt, number one in my top ten, in a roadside pond; the sudden descent of dozens of evening grosbeaks, flashing gold and white, jabbering and jostling for space on snowy feeders; dark-eyed juncos doing their rapid snow shuffle in place, hoping their busy feet will uncover a weed seed or two; a statuesque great blue heron poised motionless at the edge of the lake, watching for movements that could translate into dinner; or seeing him clamber through tree tops to his nest, maneuvering like a tightrope walker.

I remember: a silent parade of a dozen willow ptarmigan across snowy tundra, seeking out their favorite willow buds, the trail of fleur-de-lis impressions they leave in the snow delighting my sense of design; a crabapple tree in April holding eight or ten migrant warblers, flashing and flitting, lifting spirits for days. One can be overwhelmed by the living tides of migratory birds.

In the sound and song category: the unbelievably loud cackle of a pileated woodpecker as he dashes through woods, white wing patches flashing; the nostalgic, somewhat dreamy whistle of an unseen migrating white-throated sparrow on a misty spring morning, a sound that sets blood a stirring in bird watchers everywhere; the quiet whisper song of the usually raucous and often ill-mannered blue jay as he approaches his nest, his beak full of food for his incubating mate; the first cheery whistle of a cardinal on a snowy February morning in the heart of busy Chicago. Our feeders carried him through another winter.

A slow, slurred *pee a wee* from an invisible wood pewee high in treetops on a hot summer afternoon; the sudden roar of ruffed grouse wings as one takes off from almost under my feet; *rat a tat* from the woods as the downy woodpecker seeks insects in dead wood or tells a neighbor to keep his distance; when the flute-like *ee oh lay* of the wood thrush sounds through the woods, I drop everything to treasure each crystalline note. How can that little throat create such exquisite sound?

And in the courtship and mating category I remember: opening a bluebird nestbox when banding birds and finding a black-capped chickadee nest consisting of a three-inch thick mat of bright green moss carefully brought in, billful by billful; a dazzling vermillion flycatcher in a Texas copse executing huge figure eights to entrance his mate with his come-hither courtship display; holding a tiny female hummingbird in my hand, noting that even so minute a creature has a completely bare brood spot on her belly, the better to disseminate warmth to the developing embryos in her ever so tiny eggs.

Yes, there are some birds I don't love, two introduced species in particular: the noisy, drab house sparrow and the aggressive, predatory European starling. And there is one native species, the brown-headed cowbird, whose unattractive mannerisms I would wish away, because he is parasitic on other species and seriously reducing midwestern wood thrush and Kirtland's warbler populations.

Since human life began, man has been fascinated by experiences with birds, experiences which expand his sense of wonder. Even a plethora of house finches on my feeder reminds me of the endless bounty of nature and of our responsibility to conserve the world's biodiversity, everywhere threatened by the activities and needs of mankind.

December 17, 1994

Feet

The mute swan glides along the water so smoothly one assumes he is just floating. In truth, his feet and legs are moving back and forth rapidly, propelling him. With a stout body, medium-length legs set far apart, and webbed feet, movement is rapid and efficient. Feet move alternately. They are fairly large with the front three toes webbed and hind toe free, as in all members of the Anatidae family: swans, geese, and ducks. Walking on land is awkward, but paddling is graceful and easy. If you get near a flock in the water, watch closely to see how rapidly their legs move.

Loons and grebes, too, are foot propelled, but with toes more like rubber fins. Lobes (or flaps) edge each toe, instead of being connected by webs. Feet are at the back of their bodies making walking next to impossible. Don't pity them; they can dive to seventy-five feet.

Chickadees and hawks use their feet as hands to hold their food in place while taking it apart with their bills.

Birds that spend most of their time on the wing (swifts and hummingbirds) have small weak feet and are almost unable to walk.

Birds of snowy northern areas have special devices to enable them to travel safely. In autumn, a ruffed grouse grows scaly, fringe-edged appendages on the sides of its toes. These help prevent sinking into drifts. Ptarmigan of arctic climates have their toes completely covered with stiff feathers providing support and insulation. Pheasants, imported from a non-wintry area of China, have no such adaptations and often die, starved or frozen to the ground because of their inability to move in deep snow.

Great blue herons have wonderfully articulated graceful feet with long thin toes which keep them from sinking into swamps. The inside of the center toe has a unique toothed comb, useful in preening and holding onto slippery prey.

Larks and pipits, ground feeders in prairie and beach areas, have especially long hind toes to help them brace against heavy winds.

The osprey grasps its prey with thick, curved talons. Sharp pads on the underside help hold a slippery fish, its chief diet component. Other raptors have powerful talons but lack the special pads.

When birds roost, their legs have a special locking device. As they crouch, flexor tendons automatically pull toes into a fist and keep them tightly locked, all through the night if needed.

Legs and feet are almost any hue: pink, orange, blue, gray, black, or the familiar yellow of domestic chickens. The color may harmonize or contrast with the plumage.

September 23, 1993

Light as a Feather

Could you fly if you were covered with feathers? No. Why not? Because your bones are too heavy; they're not hollow like a bird's. Your body has no inflatable air sacs. It is not streamlined for smooth, effortless airflow.

Miracle is a much overused word in nature descriptions; but, truly, feathers are miracles. They enable birds to fly and help protect them from rain and cold and even from heat. Birds have more feathers in their winter plumage, and in severe cold they fluff them up with layers and layers of insulating air. Shaftless, soft down feathers keep a warm layer of air next to the skin.

Preening is an important daily chore. Feathers must be kept properly smoothed and aligned to make flight possible. For long flights, they must be in peak condition. Airplanes with wing or tail holes have trouble staying aloft and so do birds.

Oil from the uropygial gland at the base of the tail must be spread through feathers to keep them waterproofed and flexible. With only a bill as a comb, this is a time-consuming task. A bird also has fine powder-down feathers which grow continuously and break down providing a fine substance that aids in grooming and water-proofing.

All birds bathe in some way—wet or dry, in water, snow, sand, or dust—in order to keep feathers clean. Flickers, in particular, bathe in ant nests, using the ants' formic acid as an insecticide, thus keeping their plumage free of lice.

Without careful study under a high-powered lens, it's hard to realize the construction intricacies of feathers. Under magnification, hundreds of tiny barbs coming out of the quill (the basic central stalk) become visible. Each inch of shaft may have fifty barbs on one side, 100 on both sides; each barb has interlocking barbules that intersect like slats in a lattice, somewhat resembling Velcro. When a bird preens, it is making sure that all barbules are hooked, fastened together as they should be. Air cannot pass through a feather if it's zipped up.

If you have no hand lens, hold a feather to the light and squint. Do you see those barbules? They may be only a blur, because one inch of barb may contain 500 to 1,000 barbules. Figures quickly become astronomical when you multiply the number of inches of barbs by the number of barbules per inch by the number of feathers! A ruby-throated hummingbird has about 940 feathers, whereas someone once counted 25,216 on a tundra swan.

"Light as a feather" is an old saying, but a collection of feathers does have weight. For example, a bald eagle's weigh twice as much as its bones. A quill or vane is stiff and strong but also light. They say that a feather, for its weight, is stronger than any man-made material.

A product of bird's skin, the feather has no life of its own, no power of growth or renewal. It must be shed and replaced entirely. Birds molt completely at least once a year, and some twice. Geese raised for eiderdown can grow five sets of feathers annually. In molting, wing and tail feathers are shed one pair at a time, thus reducing handicaps to flight.

Because replacement consumes much energy, it usually occurs after breeding and before migration. Birds are quiet and relatively inactive during molting. Because of missing feathers and the need to save their energy, they neither sing nor display.

Ornithologists, to learn if birds rely on feathers to distinguish individuals and sexes, painted black moustaches on female flickers. Jealous males chased them as if they were other males.

I am never more aware of the complexity of feather arrangement than when handling birds about ten days old. Soft natal down covers frail little bodies while sets of feathers are popping out everywhere, all different lengths. Someday those odd looking bristly things will support flight.

Bird watchers find feathers fascinating because they use them as identifying field marks on that bird on that branch over there.

November 5, 1992

Adventures In Bird Banding

The birds—are they worth remembering?
Is flight a wonder and one wingtip a space marvel?
When will man know what birds know?
—Carl Sandburg

John James Audubon, in his early years in Pennsylvania, tied a piece of silver wire around an eastern phoebe's leg. Finding his marked bird nesting in the same cave the following year brought him great delight.

Modern bird banding procedures are much the same as Audubon's. Trapped in nets or wire cages, banders identify the birds, record age, weight, sex, and state of molt, affix a metal band of appropriate size to a leg, and then release them. The band has been stamped with identifying numbers. Data are stored in computers, available for reference and research.

The United States Fish and Wildlife Service licenses American banders to aid in monitoring population trends, migration patterns, environmental changes, and specific species studies. Additional color bands are sometimes used. Duck banding data are useful in setting bag limits for hunters.

These privileges were granted to me in 1973 to support an Audubon Breeding Bird Census study of fifty-five acres of overgrown sand prairie which had burned in a wildfire in April 1971. My project was to observe changes in populations as vegetation grew back following the fire. I learned a fascinating amount about bird physiology and habits in those hours of close observation. To work half a dozen nets was usually as much as I could manage because I had to check them regularly and at short intervals to protect the birds. Working alone, and only on weekends for the first eight years, I did not amass large amounts of data as are collected by research teams working every day and using many nets.

Every ornithological text describes migration and explains many theories of its how and why, even mentioning a migrant's ability to return to the exact site of its fledging. But to read such a fact and to hold in your hand a minute, brilliant, pulsating hooded warbler wearing the tiny band you had affixed the previous summer are two very different learnings. There are endless miracles to be observed in our natural world, but this winged mite's ability to be in my net again after a winter's sojourn in Central America excites my highest admiration. I admit that the wonder of it moved me to tears, so deeply was I touched by the miracle of return of this five-inch long creature whose brain must be less than pea size. Bird brain, indeed!

One of the most astonishing all-time banding records is that of an Arctic tern found dead on the same Maine Island where he had been banded thirty-four years earlier. At 25,000 migratory miles flown in a year, this tern weighing four ounces flew 850,000 in its lifetime.

My own records are not so astonishing, but interesting nevertheless. Veeries, a northern flicker, and gray catbirds returned to me after a southern sojourn. A rose-breasted grosbeak came into my nets after a four-year interval during which he had made four round trips to Central America. And another, banded in July 1982, revisited the next three years.

A white-throated sparrow, that bird of haunting, ethereal whistles, was banded on June fifteenth, 1985, on its way north to nest in quiet Canadian forests. It stopped off again September twenty-second on its way south to winter below the Mason-Dixon line. This supports another textbook statement. Migrants use identical stopover sites, often year after year, on their biannual migratory passages.

Records show that migrating white-crowned, white-throated, and American tree sparrows lingered as long as two weeks, while one white-throat stayed for seventeen days. I wonder if it flew nonstop to its northern nesting ground when it finally left me.

Interesting records emerge for permanent residents. A male American goldfinch, banded in August 1981, returned in May 1986 with no interim visits. A male downy woodpecker, banded in July 1981, was still around in November 1985 with one visit each intervening year. A 1980 downy returned in 1984 with two interim visits.

Vibrant black-capped chickadees were my champs; these nonmigrants were the most common species on my feeders and in my nets. A chickadee was the first bird I banded and also the last before I moved. A 1977 bandee was caught nine times before May 1979. Were my feeders its home base?

Another from November 1980 reappeared in April '86 with visits in '83 and '84. When one considers the shortness of winter days and frequency of temperatures ten, even twenty degrees below zero, a tiny chickadee's survival is remarkable. No wonder they're dashing in for seeds all day long, revving up their metabolism to sustain 111 degree body temperatures through the long cold night.

November 5, 1989

Why Populations Are Decreasing

Where are all the tiny, tiny warblers I helped band at the Kalamazoo Nature Center on September first? I wonder. Have gray and bright yellow Canada warblers that summered in the far north reached South America? Did tail-flashing magnolias and Cape Mays reach the West Indies? Did blue-winged and black-hatted Wilson's warblers make it to Panama?

These birds, each weighing as little as a butter pat, combat predators, heavy storms, turbulent winds, brightly lit skyscrapers, vast oceans, and endless miles to reach their chosen winter homes. And yet, warblers are but a fraction of the horde of Michigan's breeding birds that migrate to and from far southern lands. Swainson's thrushes fly to Argentina and rose-breasted grosbeaks may fly as far as Peru.

Then, in addition to all travel hazards they've suffered, the birds may reach their winter home to find home isn't there any more. A cherished forest was levelled for human needs of food, shelter, and clothing. Thus are biologically significant tropical forests being degraded. Just as loggers stripped Michigan of thousands of acres of white pines a century ago, neotropical forests are being laid low for mining, logging, ranching, and agricultural interests. What happens to birds that can't adapt to these changes, that can no longer find proper food and shelter? They die. And thereby hangs part of our sad tale of dramatic declines in numbers of several long-distance migrant birds.

We in the north have added to the serious hazards facing birds by things we've done to their nesting areas. Suburban sprawl, picture windows, decline of woodlots and hedgerows, air pollution, water pollution, wetlands destruction, acid rain-damaged forests, and population increases of nest-parasitic cowbirds and predatory house cats are negative factors for one species or another.

Some thrushes and warblers, whose numbers are dwindling noticeably, require forest interiors. Fragmentation of initially continuous woodlands, with roads and highways, reduces desirable nesting areas. Such division increases edge habitat and means an increase in raccoons, blue jays, and European starlings which prey on or compete with forest interior birds.

Have you ever watched starlings fight great-crested flycatchers or red-headed woodpeckers for a nesting hole? Starlings can't build holes but must nest in them. Fierce battles for occupancy seesaw back and forth for several days with starlings, in my experience, always winning.

In his discouraging book, *Where Have All the Birds Gone?*, John Terborgh analyzes in detail many threats facing our birds. His important statement for lovers of

Michigan's Kirtland's warblers warns that relaxation of the brown-headed cowbird removal program in their mating area would result in extinction of this species within five years. An increase in mechanical harvesting machinery leaves more grain in the fields. This helps support hordes of hungry cowbirds which, therefore, survive winter in greater numbers.

In an Illinois study of wood thrush nests, cited by Terborgh, Scott Robinson found thirty-seven cowbird eggs in eleven. Of thirty clutches and broods, twenty-nine had been parasitized. Said Robinson, "Wood thrushes are doing nothing but raising cowbirds." What will our summer woods be like without that sweet and plaintive wood thrush twilight song?

World population expansion exerts great pressure for development, for dams, roads, logging, agriculture, and housing, which are affecting bird life negatively. These worldwide situations make it imperative for us not only to celebrate the bird marvels we now have but also to take steps to stabilize as many situations as we can.

In *Life in the Balance*, David Rains Wallace wrote:

> If the forests that still remain on the Central American Caribbean coast and northern tip of South America are cut, and if the United States forest fragmentation continues, a North American spring as silent as Rachel Carson's vision may become a reality.

October 31, 1991

Nests

The variety in materials, structure, and location of birds' nests never ceases to amaze me. An important correlate of this variety is that the patterns are characteristic of particular species and remain the same year after year, generation after generation.

With reference books, one can almost always figure out the designer of a specific nest. A helpful volume is Hal H. Harrison's *A Field Guide to Birds' Nests* in the Peterson field guide series. At a glance, these pictures of nests found east of the Mississippi look too similar to be helpful, but careful reading will reveal materials, locations, and nesting habits. Over a fifteen-year period, he photographed 222 species at the egg-laying stage. When I met him at a Florida Christmas count, his wife was despairing at his thinking of making the same study of western bird nests: "All those ladders!"

In colonial times, barn swallows nested in caves, hollow trees, or rock crevices; they quickly adapted to man's wooden shelters, usually nesting inside, high up on rough barn walls. Their cousins, the square-tailed, white foreheaded cliff swallows, always nest outside the barn under the eaves. Only the swallows know why their choices differ.

The barn swallow gathers tiny pellets of mud of just the right consistency in its bill and painstakingly builds up the nest cup. One researcher separated a nest weighing 9 ½ ounces into its component parts: 8 ounces of clay and mud; 8 minute lumps of coal ashes; 9 bits of shells; 10 pieces of stone; 18 pieces of brick; 33 chicken feathers; 34 fragments of coal; 89 leaf stems and pieces of twigs; 114 rootlets; and 718 grass stems and fragments. Over 1,000 objects in one nest.

We had the privilege of watching mudgathering for three days one July. The first brood seemed to be helping, too, although it was frequently diverted by something to eat on the nearby sidewalk. The inch-thick mud wall was strengthened with hay, rootlets, or horse hair and the nest was lined with soft feathers. Like a tree swallow's nest, the feathers are always white, indicating ability to distinguish colors. The eggs are white with red and purple splotches, particularly at one end. Four to six eggs are laid and incubated for thirteen to seventeen days.

A house wren's nest, clever but not appealing, is nothing but bare, unyielding, uniform- length twigs worked together into a tangled mass that fills an entire bluebird box. Engineer that he is, the male not only maneuvers those hundreds of twigs through the small entrance hole, but maintains a tiny, open tunnel through the middle and down the back. The female completes his work and lays six or seven cinnamon spotted white eggs in a small grass cup. A few bits of plant down and feathers from ten to twelve kinds of birds are scattered throughout. I wonder if the plant down could be insecticidal. What other purpose could these scattered bits serve?

Water loving, steely blue tree swallows use bluebird nest boxes or tree cavities to raise their young. Their rather thin constructions are of dried grasses placed in a conventional circular form, only slightly cupped. A distinguishing characteristic is the fifty to one hundred white chicken or gull feathers lining the cup, ends curling over the eggs. I wonder how and why that pattern developed and how long swallows have to hunt, and how far they have to go to find feathers. She builds the nest; does she alone forage for feathers? Four to six lovely pure white eggs are incubated only by the female for thirteen to sixteen days.

A killdeer's nest, little more than a scrape on open ground or gravel with a few pebbles or blades of grass for a liner, often is hard to find because of clever camouflage. I've seen one in the gravel beside a tennis court; we could locate the nest only when the adult bird rose from it. Egg mottling matched its surroundings perfectly. Similarly, on pebbled flats at Bear River Refuge in Utah, we couldn't find the eggs from six feet away. Thus do ground-nesting birds try to protect themselves. The young, covered with buffy-brown down, hatch from large greenish-buff, heavily spotted eggs after twenty-five days of incubation by both parents. They run around and feed themselves right away, precocial as ornithologists say. In about three weeks, wing feathers have grown out and are strong enough to sustain flight.

Some killdeer nest on flat gravel roofs. Such locales present serious problems to the newly hatched chicks, which are unable either to fly or find food on rooftops.

Last year, a mallard duck laid her eggs in oak leaves that filled a shallow depression in a partially dead ground juniper right by the house. Each morning, the pair of ducks appeared, walking up from the lake and meandering along, slowly approaching the site. She finally came to the nest; he sashayed around a while and then disappeared. Day 1 she laid an egg and left. Day 2 she laid a second and stayed an hour. Day 3, yet another, staying an hour and a half, leaving light greenish-buff eggs completely exposed. By day 8 there were eight, all cold, but protected with bits of fluffy down which she plucked from her breast. After laying ten, four disappeared one night. She gave up and I never saw her again. Had she stayed, she would have started the twenty-three to twenty-nine day incubation period after laying the last one.

The most exquisite nest I have ever seen is a little goldfinch's cup knocked out of a tree in a summer storm. It was constructed entirely of thistledown fibers, carefully matted and shaped. As well as being soft and downy, comfortable and protective, it was a lustrous work of art.

May 13, 1995

Pied-billed Grebes

Now you see him, now you don't. The pied-billed grebe has a unique ability to sink slowly in the water at will. He expels air from his plumage and air sacs throughout his body, submerging gradually as specific gravity decreases. Does he move his feet to help the descent? Who knows? Once submerged, he is foot propelled and swims away as he pleases, sometimes with just bill and eyes showing. It's always a guess where he will emerge again.

A primeval order of bird little changed in some 80 million years, grebes are related to loons on the avian family tree. There are seventeen species worldwide, and six occur in North America. Five are localized in distribution while the pied-billed is found throughout the continent.

The bird is twelve- to fifteen-inches long, but somehow looks smaller. He is compact, round-bodied, and without visible sign of a tail. Brown in overall appearance, his neck is short and thick supporting a small rounded head with a notably thick, blunt bill. His name comes from a black stripe completely circling the bill. This mark and a black patch on the chin and upper throat disappear in winter.

In southern Michigan's numerous small ponds and lakes, the pied-billed is the most common grebe, but shyness prevents frequent sightings. They like shallow freshwater habitats, are rarely seen in saltwater, and are considered both territorial and aggressive.

When feeding, or alarmed, the grebe shows off his diving prowess. His powerful wings mean he dives easily and quickly, seeming to leap from the surface. This skill gives him the nickname of hell diver.

Like all members of his genus, the pied-billed has lobed toes with partial webbing surrounding them. These flexible webs act like feathering action of a canoe paddle, helping him steer. Feet are placed well back on his body, making him awkward on land. He rarely is seen flying, but does manage to migrate south to get away from ice locked lakes. A few remain in Michigan if ponds stay open. The majority return in early or mid-March, feeding on tadpoles, small fish, and wetland insects.

In *The Atlas of Breeding Birds of Michigan*, Robert W. Storer wrote, "fluctuating water levels, wave action, and predation...are the most frequent causes of nesting failure." The floating nest found in lakes, ponds, and extensive marshes in April and May is anchored to rooted vegetation and is well-hidden. Constructed of soggy old sedges, rushes, and cattail leaves, the perfect bowl holds four to eight whitish eggs. Incubation is for twenty-three days. Eggs are covered carefully with debris when the sitting parent leaves.

Pert hatchlings are precocial, able to walk and swim

at birth. Young are zebra-striped in brown and white and sport an orange chevron on their crown, a distinctive mark which disappears quickly. If danger threatens, they scramble on mother's back and she swims away with them, a rare sight to see. She may dive with them clinging to her if necessary.

The pied-billed grebe's distinctive call, heard only in the breeding season, is a loud whinny, a series of a dozen notes, slowing down to a repeated *cow cow cow*. The call is heard more often than the bird is seen.

Clownish charms and unique skills of this little diver serve to remind us again of our responsibility to keep some undisturbed wetlands as part of the Michigan scene. Otherwise, the present general decline of this charmer will continue.

May 6, 1993

The Grouse Family in Michigan

Michigan's northern forests are graced by the presence of three resident members of the grouse family: spruce, sharp-tailed, and ruffed. These heavy-bodied, chicken-like birds have short, rounded wings which sustain a quick fluttery flight.

The rare spruce grouse, as its name implies, is found only in northern areas of short-needled conifers, especially in or near black spruce swamps. Evergreen tips and buds are his staple food. In winter he may eat as much as four ounces of needles in one day. This grouse likes mixed areas of spruce and jack pine near small openings where blueberries, bracken fern, and reindeer lichen make good nibbling.

Primarily a northern wilderness species, only eighteen townships in Michigan are reported to have fool hens, as old-timers called the bird. Rare and protected since 1915, this grouse is unusually tame and trusting and can be approached closely.

Sharp-tailed grouse are also limited in Michigan. At present, nesting has been confirmed in fourteen townships. An open grassland habitué, this bird has actually profited by earlier clearing of large acreages of coniferous forest, but now its habitats are threatened with reforestation and succession. Some public land rangers in the Upper Peninsula are carrying out management practices that will help maintain or increase populations.

Like their cousins, the prairie chickens, male sharp-taileds gather at dawn on communal display grounds to bob and strut, run and leap, with red combs and orange-tipped black tail feathers stiffly erect and purplish neck sacs inflated. This frenzied activity, accompanied by a low hooting which sounds like blowing across the top of an empty bottle, not only attracts females for mating but also establishes dominance.

Largely vegetarian, sharp-taileds feed on leaves, buds, and flowers. Like spruce grouse, they nest in a shallow depression in the ground, where the female lays five to seven eggs. Her cryptic plumage coloration helps camouflage the nest. Like all gallinaceous birds, newly hatched chicks are fully feathered and able to care for themselves. They peck first at insects (beetles, flies, snails, spiders, ants) but soon turn to a vegetarian diet.

Southern Michigan's member of Galliformes is the year-round resident ruffed grouse, the brown drummer bird of woods and overgrown pastures. A great favorite of hunters who bag over 100,000 a year, this bird can hold its own if its aspen habitat is available. A quiet, unobtrusive walker on forest floors, it often alarms us, when flushed, by a sudden burst into full flight with a roar of wings.

During courtship in April, the male sits on a chosen

drumming log, fan tail erect, and beats the air with his wings at a rapidly increasing tempo. Compressed air makes the far-carrying sound. He does not share in any group activity in a special dancing area.

In winter, tough scaly fringes grow on toe edges of the feet of ruffed grouse, serving as unique snow shoes. These drop off in spring. Dried fruits (greenbrier, blueberry, apple, cherry, grape and strawberry) are important in winter diets along with essential aspen and conifer buds. Like willow ptarmigan, these grouse will spend cold winter nights in a snow bank.

This species comes in two color phases, gray and red. Differences show mainly in the color of tail bands and seem to occur randomly, without relation to age, sex, or season.

Hawks, owls, and foxes are the natural predators of all upland game birds.

November 5, 1994

Wild Turkeys

When Mexico fell to Cortez in the early 1500s, this country's wild turkey had already been domesticated. Spanish explorers soon introduced the bird to Europe where it became established as a barnyard fowl. Wild turkeys originally were abundant in southern Michigan's lower peninsula. Their meat and feathers were important to both Indians and early settlers, but habitat destruction and overhunting extirpated the species by 1900.

Starting in 1954, turkeys were reintroduced as a wild game species, with the state's Department of Natural Resources determining hunting limits. In 1991, the total population was estimated at 52,000 in the north and 8,000 farther south. In the last year, I've seen small flocks along Route 131 near Cadillac, in Fort Custer National Cemetery, and in Gobles woodlands.

The domestic turkey, now raised by the millions in the United States, is fatter than its wild cousin and his tail is white-tipped rather than rusty. Hundreds of standard breeds have been developed to provide our tables with leaner, tastier meat. In the wild, the strong, long-legged turkey roams forest clearings and wood edges in search of grape, juniper, and dogwood fruits, insects and small amphibians, seeds, beech and hickory nuts, and especially acorns, a staple food, which he eats whole. Can you imagine one bird's crop with 221 large acorns?

A full-grown male consumes a pound of food at a time. Rhythmic contractions of his muscular gizzard crush nutshells in a matter of hours; even a hickory nut is in bits after thirty-one hours. An Italian scholarly priest discovered that a turkey gizzard could grind up steel needles and surgical lancets.

Males, which can be as much as four feet long, have bare bluish heads spotted with warty growths and unmistakable strange red fleshy wattles on their throats and neck fronts. Their heavy bodies are covered with iridescent copper brown feathers, variously striped and barred. The paler, slimmer female is usually not longer than three feet and lacks large wattles. A black beard on the breast is apparent in males and some females. The male's one-inch spur on the back of his leg is used in courtship fighting.

When I first went a-birding in the early fifties, we hunted for wild turkeys at Aransas, Texas. We had given up and were leaving the refuge when suddenly, around the exit bend, appeared a flock of eight or ten with huge tails all fanned out and waving gently as the birds strutted slowly along, an unforgettable sight.

Although the bird is a weak flyer, running rather than flying to avoid danger, he, like other Galliformes, roosts in trees at night and in bad weather.

The male makes a familiar *gobble gobble*, especially in

the morning, when he wishes to gather his harem from roost sites. His deep bass sound can be heard a mile away. A female's cluck is more like a chicken's. Both sexes have alarm notes.

Turkeys are adaptable to various climate conditions as long as food is available. They come regularly to bird feeding areas for cracked corn. In winter when the snow is deep, they have been known to fast for a week without apparent harm.

Mating season displays are notable. Polygamous males strut and gobble, before hens, with erect tails fully fanned and stiff wing quills dragging the ground. In the *Life Book of Birds*, Roger Tory Peterson wrote:

> Wild turkey gobblers on promenade pay more attention to each other than to the hens. Shoulder to shoulder the big toms strut... . In the fever pitch of their rivalry, their naked heads turn bright blue and their wattles become gorged with blood; when one bird gobbles they all gobble simultaneously. When a hen is ready to mate, she must take the initiative, literally, prostrating herself before the tom turkey of her choice before he will allow himself to be diverted from his self-centered pomposity.

Hens make their nests in scratched out hollows in the ground under shrubby cover where eight to fifteen buff-colored spotted eggs are laid. The young can fly short distances within two weeks, but stay close to mother until fall, feeding on high protein insects.

Audubon painted the wild turkey as plate number one in *The Birds of America*.

November 25, 1993

Tu Whit Tu Whoo in Kalamazoo

Tu whit tu whoo. Who cooks for you all? Of all the eerie calls of all the local owls, this hooting of the northern barred is my favorite. It's hard to believe that it's really a bird making those nine notes when you hear that impressive sound close-by. So unreal. So penetrating.

A family of barred owls lived near me and one often hooted from the big pine just outside my bedroom window. It was a scary but delightful experience to be wakened by that call of the wild only ten feet from my bed.

In addition to the familiar *who cooks for you all?* Allen Eckert, in *The Owls of North America*, described numerous other calling patterns of this most vocal one as "weird shrieks, screams, cries, trillings, grumbles, squeals and hootings....deep chucklings, harsh laughing sounds, maniacal gibberings and gabblings, disconsolate mutterings, howls and yells...even a disconcerting human-like scream of pure agony."

Barred owls are lookalikes and close relatives of the endangered spotted owl. We have heard much about this bird over whose future existence the lumbering of ancient western forests has caused so much furor.

In the Kalamazoo area the northern barred is listed as an uncommon permanent resident. You can hear his far-carrying hooting in undisturbed, deep, dark woods along the river bottom. He responds readily to taped or human imitations. Both male and female call, she with a higher pitch.

You may feel more than a little conspicuous when trying to learn to imitate owl calls. Such mastery adds much to your birding repertoire and is worth the self-conscious feeling of stupidity. Young people are adept at learning to imitate the barred owl, but they shouldn't practice if there's a family dog. If you call at night, perhaps on the edge of two owls' territories, you may get an excited response with an astounding variety of gabbling and cackling.

Permanent residents of swamp woods where squirrels, crayfish, frogs, mice, and rabbits are hunted, barred owls' gray-brown camouflage is seen more readily in winter when trees are bare. They perch immobile, close to tree trunks for long periods, even the entire day, unless disturbed by harassing crows and jays who think taunting them is A one fun. Usually owls won't move if nests are nearby, unless to fly at a crow that gets too close. If there is no nest, the bored owl eventually takes off silently, pursued by raucous crows.

These birds have smooth yet puffy round heads. Their faces are flat with appealing brown eyes, rather than yellow like other owls. Eyes are forward facing and immovably fixed in their sockets, requiring movement of the entire head to change viewpoints. Necks are extremely flexible, permitting turns of almost a full circle. Vision is keen, particularly at night, but also by day.

Barred owls have four or five concentric circles of light and dark feathers around their eyes. It is thought these discs act as parabolic reflectors to assist in detecting the exact source of a sound, a great help in dusk and dawn hunting times. Invisible ears are cavities in lower sides of the head covered with loose-ribbed feathers that can spread to form funnels. Hearing is extremely acute; ears are asymmetrical in size and shape to help in locating sound. So keen is this sense that, like barn owls, they can hunt by sound alone.

The yellow beak is wickedly hooked, efficient for tearing flesh. Barring on the big neck ruff gives this owl its name. The belly is striped vertically and the back is brown with white spots. Plumage colors of male and female are identical, but she is always larger. Crow-size and weighing about a pound, the northern barred looks bigger due to its heavy, dense plumage and upright doll-like posture when perched.

The noiseless and buoyant moth-like flight, characteristic of owls, interests scientists. Movements of the barred are dignified and deliberate. It's amazing to watch this bulky-appearing, short-winged bird maneuver skillfully through dense branches, not flapping a wing, just tipping enough to prevent collision, gliding upward to alight on a branch.

Feathers are soft, but close examination shows that the long primary ones have an extremely fine fringe, called fluting, on edges. Fluting, which reduces air resistance and makes possible silent flight, is easily seen if you hold a feather to the light. It resembles serrations on a saw blade's edge.

Northern barred owls nest in tree cavities, twenty to forty feet up, often using the same nest for many years. Courtship, beginning in late winter, is accompanied by complex posturing and bobbing poses and an incredible variety of sounds. Two pure white eggs are laid on the practically bare floor of the hollow. Egg-laying and subsequent hatching occur at intervals of a week or even two. This delay is a protective device against loss of both babies in face of a severe storm or unseasonable food shortages.

Favorite foods are small mammals which are captured with powerful sharp talons and carried away in the beak. On perching, the owl shuffles the prey until it is in a proper position to be swallowed whole. Undigestible bones and fur are compacted into pellets and ejected orally, about one to three mucus-slickened pellets per night. Birds as large as crows and slow-water fish are taken, even lizards, turtles, and snakes.

Life span of wild northern barred owls is known to be as high as eight years, in zoos well over twenty.

One April day in a high wind a large dead maple, whose trunk was decorated with a *Hydnum* the previous autumn, broke off at the point where this mushroom grew, exposing a barred owl's nest. I looked for the owls, finding only a dead baby on the ground. Less than a week old, it was covered with long, fine white down, its egg tooth was still present, and its eyes were sealed. It weighed under two ounces and was about four inches long. I cried for the loss of this beautiful thing. The previous year this nest fledged a handsome baby.

One May twilight, friends watched parents of a two-week-old barred owl settle near their nest, exchange much babbling and cackling; then each adult groomed the other at length.

Throughout time, man has been in awe of owls attributing to them wisdom and supernatural powers. Appearance in a city signified hard times ahead. Feathers were used in incantations. But for us a northern barred owl represents avian beauty and mystery at its best. *Who cooks for you, who cooks for you all?* is heard from the Nature Center's beechwoods, and is answered. Yes, Kalamazoo still has wild places for wild things.

January 8, 1991

Hummy

If we were to rank all miracles we see in nature, surely hummingbirds would head many a list. Unbelievably minute, they charm all watchers.

Their motto seems to be dart-glitter-flit and dart-glitter-flit again. Known only to the New World, there are some 342 species, 163 in Ecuador alone. Fourteen are found in the western United States although east of the Mississippi River only one flies among scarlet flowers, the ruby-throated.

Audubon described a hummingbird as a "glittering fragment of the rainbow." When light conditions are right, the adult male's throat truly glows, is luminescent, and reminds me of stained glass colors at Chartres. A quick turn of his head and the throat goes black, only to flash red again momentarily.

Both sexes have shiny, iridescent, metallic green backs and pure white underparts. First year males' throats are white, overlaid with minute black feather tips. Females' throats and outer tail tips are white.

They feed on flower nectar, small insects, and spiders, obtaining from these the energy necessary to support their 200-times-a-second wing beat. South American scientists clock their heart beats at 1,440 per minute. A human doing aerobic exercise records a mere 110 per minute. Hummies must eat every 15 minutes to sustain life and daily consume enough to equal their body weight. At night their temperatures drop. They breathe 50 to 100 times less oxygen, inducing a deep torpor.

So tiny are they, four inches long at best and one tenth of an ounce, it would take 150 to make a pound. I'm not one of the privileged few licensed to band them, but when they occasionally get in my net I marvel at them closeup. They are fearless and just sit on my hand, tiny feet barely felt. Minute legs and feet reduce overall weight, an important consideration in so small a being. His bill, so awkward looking during meticulous preening or when feeding young, protects the extrusible tongue as it darts into flowers.

Hummingbirds can fly upside down and are the only birds that fly backwards. When hovering, their wings beat so rapidly they appear to be motionless. These tiny wings go through remarkable 180 degree revolutions to accomplish these aeronautical triumphs. The hummers perch for long periods between spells of flight. They are fiercely territorial, protecting nest, favorite perch, and nectar site with vigorous chases and aerial battles, sometimes even with jays or starlings. Ruby-throated's courtship displays are spectacular, amazing to experience. The female sits out of sight while the male dive-bombs repeatedly in big loopy U's above her, his aerobatics resembling a pendulum's swing.

Essentially voiceless, the bird makes clicking sounds. Its name refers to the gentle buzz of wings.

The one- to two-inch downy nest, placed on a lichen-covered branch, is camouflaged with lichens and holds two navy-bean sized eggs. The hatchling is less than a half inch long.

Feeding on sugar water feeders in our yards, dazzling antics are endlessly fascinating to watch. A friend, Clyde Fields, was eating watermelon on his back porch one summer day when a passing hummy landed on the red fruit. The next day, he rigged his camera attachments and, using a cable release, got a fine closeup of bird, fruit, and Clyde. He titled it *Sharing*.

And don't forget, when a thumb-size ruby-throated leaves for South America in fall, this wee being makes an extraordinary 500-mile nonstop flight across the Gulf of Mexico from the tip of Florida to the coast of Yucatan. Miracle? Yes.

June 10, 1993

Red-bellied Woodpecker

A common permanent resident of southern Michigan woodlands, the red-bellied woodpecker is a creature whose name is a strange misfit. This handsome bird's red coloring is more conspicuous on its head than on its belly. Also, the color of its belly, what little there is, is really more orange than red. One can't help wondering how such names originate. The scientific name, *Melanerpes carolinus*, given it by Linnaeus in 1758, tells us only that it is a "black creeper-like bird" first identified in Carolina.

Easily detected by its ringing, rolling *churr*, the noisy male has a flaming scarlet crown and nape. Black and white zebra stripes on the back, tail, and wings and a tinged area of tangerine shades on his belly are characteristic. Red on the female is confined to the back of her head.

The bird is familiar to many of us because it readily comes to feeders. With its unique two-toes-in-front and two-toes-in-back foot design, it clamps awkwardly to suet feeders or stands flatfooted on a platform feeder to pick up sunflower seeds or cracked corn bits. When I lived in the country, I always had a wintering male or female, but never both. The winter feeding territory apparently had to be so large there was room for only one bird. As soon as courtship time arrived, a bird of the other sex appeared and the pair fed all summer, even bringing their scrawny young to the feeder as summer wore on.

In the wild, it hammers on trunks or branches with its heavy chisel-tipped bill, just like its relatives. Larvae of wood-boring insects are its favorite food, but it also eats many other insects. When acorns or beech nuts are found, they are stored in any handy hole or crevice. Its close cousin, the comic appearing acorn woodpecker of the Far West, actually makes special holes in trees or power poles for storing treasures. One giant sycamore in California had 20,000 acorns stored in it, each in its own specially drilled cubbyhole.

In addition to eating ants, beetles, grasshoppers, crickets, and caterpillars, these woodpeckers flycatch in the air, a delightful sight to observe. They also eat oranges, cherries, and apples and take peanut butter bits stuffed in holes in logs as fast as a blue jay does.

One thing that has always fascinated me about birds is the nature, number, and variety of feathers on a single individual as well as wide differences in color and number between species. A ruby-throated hummingbird collected in June had 940 feathers while a red-bellied taken in April had 3,665 with wide variations in texture, length, color, and function.

Red-bellieds are ten inches long, about the size of a hairy woodpecker, and weigh three ounces. They may live as long as eight to ten years, with one bander's unusual record of twenty years, eight months. They range east of the Rockies and as far north as central Michigan and southern New England and are slightly migratory in the northern part of their range.

Like its relatives, the red-bellied has short, heavy legs, extremely sharp claws, stiff central tail feathers, an extensible tongue fringed or barbed along its edges, and a strong, graceful, undulating flight.

First indications of territoriality and of courtship activity occur in early March. By late April a deep woods nest site has been chosen. A twelve-inch deep hole is then excavated by both adults, and four to five fine-grained, dull white eggs are laid. Red-bellieds occasionally nest in bird houses, if they are deep enough, with a two-inch diameter hole. In woods, they excavate their nests in softer wooded trees such as maple, elm, basswood, or poplar.

Incubation, carried out by both parents, is for eleven and a half days; young are born blind, naked, and totally helpless. Parents feed them in the nest for more than three weeks and keep close track of them for another six after fledging. This is an unusually long period of dependence. Once the young leave the nest, the family moves from deep woods to forest edges.

As with other large hole-nesting birds, European starlings are fierce nest site competitors of the red-bellied. No sooner has it finished excavating than the aggressive starling, in a two- or three-day series of battles, forces the woodpecker to abandon its work. Maybe the only strategy that will save the woodpeckers is for them to start nestings after the starling has finished.

Woodpeckers have no true song but each species has its own distinctive call notes and ritual tapping and drumming sequences for communicating location, territorial claims, and courtship cues.

October 2, 1989

Red-headed Woodpecker

One of America's best-known and most beautiful birds is the red-headed woodpecker. The brilliant head, coal black back, wings, and tail, and shining white wing patches make a striking pattern as it flashes through woods or flies parallel to country roads calling *kweer kweer* loudly. Its range is over much of North America, east of the Rockies.

Their preference for farmland edges and open woods keeps them where we can observe and hear them easily. This woodpecker reached its highest numbers after Dutch elm disease decimated large acreages of forest. Although not so common now, it still ranges throughout lower Michigan and occasionally in the Upper Peninsula. In some years, a few birds stay through winter, depending on the adequacy of beech nut and acorn crops. They come to bird feeders for suet, sunflower seeds, and cracked corn and hunt for insect larvae in decaying wood.

Red-headeds, like acorn woodpeckers, store nuts and acorns, even angleworms, in any crevice, knothole, or cranny they can find. They also tear open ears of corn and eat several tender, milky grains. Besides nuts, they feed on fruits, berries, and insects.

Many human factors cause hardships for this species. In today's heavy, fast automobile traffic, even on country roads, red-headeds endanger their own existence. They dart into roadways in pursuit of flying insects or slowly fly up from roadside anthills. Their populations also are threatened by loss of habitat: elimination of hedgerows for farming; extensive cutting of firewood for fuel; and control of fire in our woodlands. Removal of dead wood from woodlots also reduces nest sites and potential food supplies. Competition from other cavity nesters, such as the starling, limits nesting success. When circumstances favor, they are long-lived. One bird banded in Battle Creek was found dead there ten years later.

Four to seven eggs are laid in nest cavities that may be eight to twenty inches deep. After twelve days of incubating by both parents, the eggs hatch and nestlings are sightless and featherless for eight to ten days. Parents alternate the tasks of incubating eggs and brooding young until feathers grow out. Both develop brood patches, clear areas on bellies, enabling them to keep eggs and young warm by touching them with their skin, sharing their own body heat.

When a parent enters a nest headfirst with food, it prods its blind baby on a protrusion on the side of its face. The little mouth opens so soft insects can be crammed in. The adult then taps the nestling's rear to signal excretion time. The white, semisoft fecal sac is carried off and dropped, often over water. Good nest sanitation is important because of long occupancy. On occasion, a stressed parent swallows the sac to use undigested food.

After thirty days, the young fledge. But parental duties aren't over. They still spend weeks supervising the juveniles' efforts to forage for themselves. On emergence from the nest hole, fledglings have brownish-black heads and black stripes across white wing patches. The fully red head feathers emerge by the following April, but black wing stripes stay until the end of the second year.

Red-headeds' claws have incredibly sharp, needle-pointed tips which leave unmistakable autographs on the fingers of birdbanders. Their tongues are extensible and barbed along the ends so they can impale insects quickly and firmly.

Generally, these and other woodpeckers are beneficial to landowners and are the main providers of abandoned nesting cavities for other wildlife. However, many complain about their drilling on the sides of houses. If they are drilling on yours, it usually means one of two things. Either it has been chosen as a territorial marker (use flashy mobiles which move and make noise in the wind to discourage them) or it has insect pests. In the latter case, this enjoyable group of birds can actually provide you with hints of unseen problems.

June 11, 1989

Blue Jay

When a raucous *jay jay jay* echoes through the woodland, we humans pay little attention but all woodland denizens sense that this scream is an alarm worth observing. The blue jay is ever watchful of danger and all wildlife seems to take its screams seriously.

In writing of birds at Trail Wood, his retirement home, Edwin Way Teale noted that he had seen muskrats, rabbits, squirrels, and loons far out on a lake react to a jay's warning.

With noisy ways and bright, striking plumage this permanent resident is well-known to everyone, bird watcher or not. This is not a bird we go out looking for, armed with binoculars, telescopes, and bird books. This is a bird we've simply always known. Does anyone remember his first one? Probably not.

His scientific name, *Cyanocitta cristata*, describes him well because it means blue-crested chattering bird. The handsome western Steller's jay is another member of that genus. North American crows, ravens, magpies, and nutcrackers, close Corvidae relatives of our jay, have evolved a highly developed intelligence.

Jays are common inhabitants of parks and suburban areas east of the Rocky Mountains. In southern Michigan the same birds probably remain in oak and pine woods year-round, but those from farther north tend to move south for the winter. When they do migrate, they move by day. On April 28, 1981, 2,210 were observed flying eastward along the Lake Michigan shore east of Gary, Indiana. Raymond J. Adams, Jr., research director of the Kalamazoo Nature Center, reports that fall migrant blue jays fly southwest through the area in late September and throughout October.

These birds are omnivorous. However, they prefer vegetable matter, enjoying corn, acorns, and beech nuts if they can find them, but eat nearly all wild seeds and berries. A fondness for peanuts has been observed. They finish off with beetles, grasshoppers, frogs, salamanders, also small birds.

Frequently, blue jays use bird baths and even sun bathe.

Have you noticed that a blue jay seems fearless, often flying directly to a bird feeder, not making careful reconnaissance stops along the way as chickadees or cardinals do? Smaller birds scatter quickly when he swoops down, because his assaultive manners do not match his stunning appearance. A jay stops at a feeder long enough to gulp sixteen or eighteen sunflower seeds and vanishes in a blue flash. What does he do with all those seeds? Swallow them whole? Does his digestive system dissolve the outer shell? Does he poke them away somewhere in a secret cache or bury them in the ground where, if uneaten, they may sprout later?

Possessed of a variety of calls in addition to its shrill, harsh alarm note, the bird is an accomplished mimic, especially of hawks. During nesting season, both sexes, similar in plumage, become secretive, furtive, quiet, indeed almost silent. Four to six eggs are laid in a bulky nest made of twigs, moss, leaves, and, frequently, trash.

In hand, bird banders find blue jays amazingly limp and supine, without sound or movement. Gone is the brash bravado, but the flashing black eye remains ever watchful.

Because blue jays are known to eat other birds' nestlings, they often are chased by their neighbors. I remember watching a pair of cardinals boxing a jay into a large lilac bush for an entire morning, attacking fiercely whenever he tried to escape.

Jays can live to fifteen years. They often are devoted mates and good parents. Males, like the male cardinal, feed females during courtship and at the nest. Edward H. Forbush tells of jays not only feeding and guarding an old, partly blind jay, but also leading it to water. Who would have expected compassion from this often aggressive intruder?

December 19, 1991

American Crows

The word crow appears in our life and language in many guises. The Crow tribe were Plains Indians, also called Absarokas. "To eat crow" is to accept what one has fought against. "As the crow flies" is to go in a straight line. A crowbar is a tool for prying. "Crows' feet," a figurative term applied to those things we don't want around our eyes, is found even in Chaucer's *Canterbury Tales*. Evergreen crowberry is a small alpine shrub much like cranberry. A crow's nest is a high lookout on a sailing vessel's mast. Crowfoot is a common name for the buttercup flower family. A rooster crows, as does a young baby.

"Black as a crow" refers to the deep glossy black feathers of a large, clever bird known to almost every one: the American crow. These noisy birds are so common that we tend to ignore them as they strut around our yards or fly above corn fields. The hoarse *caw caw* is a sound most often heard in their favorite open country habitat.

Breeding throughout the United States and much of Canada, the bird's largest numbers occur in the midwest, or during winter in the south. They generally are permanent residents, but some northern birds drift south to escape cold. Winter flocks can number as high as 200,000 where food is available. Close relations, fish and northwestern crows, occupy Florida and Puget Sound niches whereas cousin common raven takes over higher and colder habitats. There are seventeen members of the family in North America.

Crows are omnivorous. They eat anything, dead or alive, plant or animal. When driving in the country, you will often scare up one who has been feeding on a traffic-killed mammal or bird. Insects, spiders, crustaceans, frogs, snakes, earthworms, grains, and seeds are all to its taste. In coastal areas they, like gulls, carry shellfish high in the air and cannily drop them to crack them open. They are fearless scavengers at garbage dumps and live all winter on waste grain in farmers' fields. The landscape changes from forests to fields have led to small but significant increases in eastern populations, a fact documented by breeding bird surveys. Unfortunately, these birds are also nest predators, eating both eggs and young of other birds. Like owls, they cough up pellets of indigestible parts of seeds and bones. Crows, which travel as much as thirty to fifty miles in a day in search of food, are economically useful to farmers for the incredible number of insects they consume.

Feathers are entirely black, with a slight purplish sheen. Stout beak, heavy legs, and large claws are black, too. A full-grown crow is from seventeen to twenty-one inches long and weighs about a pound. He walks, not hops, on the ground.

They have a unique courtship dance made up of stiff

bowing and puffing out of feathers. Devoted mates, they bill each other's plumage like doves. Although crows exhibit much gregarious flock behavior, especially hassling and mobbing owls, they are not colonial nesters, preferring to conduct family life without interruptions by neighbors. Nests are built twenty to sixty feet up in tree crotches, often evergreens.

A pattern of easy adaptation to surroundings, so apparent in feeding choices, is evident again in the opportunistic choice of nest materials. The large, substantial basket is of branches and twigs, lined with bark fibers, moss, grass, twine, feathers, rags, wool, leaves, animal hair, or seaweeds. Three to eight oval eggs are bluish or grayish green with a slight gloss. Incubation, possibly by both parents, is for eighteen days. The young are able to fly after a month as coddled nestlings. Because the nest is firmly built, it is often used in subsequent years by long-eared owls or hawks.

Banded wild birds as old as fourteen years have been found, while those in captivity may live to twenty or more, still sprightly and sparkling of eye. Crows at the Nature Center, which cannot survive in the wild because of permanent injuries, were adults when they arrived in 1987 and 1988. A veterinarian examining them recently found them in good health.

The crows' deep, steady wing beat, almost as if they were rowing, is characteristic. They do not glide or soar except in strong updrafts or when descending.

Calls vary widely from the familiar basic *caw*. After studying voice tapes, two scholars described twenty-three different ones. They noted that crows mimic the squawk of a hen, the cry of a child, and the whine of a dog. In captivity, they learn to imitate human speech and laughter. John K. Terres wrote:

> They have evolved the highest degree of intelligence among birds. Experiments with captive American crows showed that they can count to three or four, are keen, wary birds, are good at solving puzzles and at performing astonishing feats of memory, and quickly learn to associate various noises and symbols with food.

Henry Ward Beecher once said that if men wore feathers, most of them wouldn't be clever enough to be crows.

November 6, 1990

Black-capped Chickadees

Among year-round residents, black-capped chickadees receive high ratings for charm and personality. Smart of plumage and quick of movement, they dash into feeders and away again to find a place to crack their seeds. They anchor them between their long, thin toes on tree branches and hammer out kernels with direct blows, somehow avoiding their toes.

These birds are contagiously gay and friendly. Fearless, they can be tamed to feed from your hand or light on your head. I prefer my birds wild, but some people, especially children, derive great pleasure from taming them. In hand, a five-inch-long chickadee seems weightless and inert; set free, its high energy never flags; alert black eyes never stop watching. Both sexes have gray backs, black caps and bibs, and white cheeks.

Chickadees are the despair of bird banders who use mist nets. The birds tangle their long, strong toes in fine nylon mesh, clamping them firmly around each other. The minute a bander frees two toes and turns to two others, the first two are enmeshed again. Four hands are useful for freeing chickadees.

Black-capped chickadees nest in tree holes four to ten feet above the ground. Because their small, thin bills, though sharp, aren't heavy enough to hew out chips except in soft wood, they use knotholes or holes previously chiseled by woodpeckers. They also nest in man-made structures, often in boxes on a bluebird trail.

It's delightful to find a bluebird box about one-third filled with a mattress of freshly harvested bright green moss. A chickadee is nesting. Only moss, a few feathers, and some plant down or rabbit fur is used; the babies' bed is soft and warm.

Tiny whitish eggs, daintily spotted with reddish brown at one end, are incubated by the female for twelve to thirteen days. Six or eight little dynamos are chic and perky at three or four days. How can the diminutive parents gather enough food to keep that many mouths filled? During the early days after hatching, only soft-bodied insects are fed; insects have more protein than seeds.

By ten days, nestlings are large enough to be banded without danger of encouraging premature fledging. At fourteen to eighteen days, the saucy young are ready to fly with full-grown feathers, indistinguishable from their parents. There are no sexual differences in plumage. After fledging, the young remain dependent on their parents for three to four weeks.

They forage industriously and acrobatically over tree branches, feeding on insects and eggs. An entomologist said that a chickadee destroyed 5,500 canker worm eggs in one day.

The familiar cheerful *chicka dee dee* is heard constantly

all day, all year long. An easily imitated, plaintive, minor whistle *fee be* is heard often in spring. A love song? If disturbed while on the nest, females hiss like a snake.

Despite their diminutive size, chickadees endure even the coldest weather. No fair-weather friends, they appear at feeders in dawn's earliest light, preceded only by northern cardinals. In cold weather they become totally round, fluffing feathers to almost twice their normal size, thereby trapping air as insulation. One morning at twenty-five degrees below zero, I saw inflated chickadees covered with hoar-frost crystals, dazzling in the sunlight. They seemed unperturbed by the bitter cold, continuing their usual feeding activities.

Chickadees at rest often shiver for short periods, converting muscular energy into heat. They eat constantly during short winter days in order to replace the energy lost in keeping warm. On cold nights, they enter a torpid condition. Body temperatures drop twenty degrees as pulse and breathing slow thirty percent. They lose as much as ten percent of body weight overnight, making early breakfast mandatory.

> Piped a tiny voice near by,
> Gay and polite, a cheerful cry—
> Chick-chickadeedee! saucy note
> Out of sound heart and merry throat,
> As if it said, "Good-day, good Sir!
> Fine afternoon, old passenger!
> Happy to meet you in these places
> Where January brings few faces."
> —Ralph Waldo Emerson

January 30, 1992

Nuthatches

Among the most common and vibrant of year-round birds are nuthatches, the Sittidae.

Boldly patterned with blue back, black crown and nape, white underparts, and touches of rust on its flanks, the white-breasted is a loyal member of the feeder club. A bright black eye stands out in contrast to a white face. Male and female are similar, but she's smaller and grayer overall. Differences may not be noticeable unless they're together. Outer tail feathers have white corners visible only in flight. Some ornithologists theorize that these flashing white triangles are camouflage to confuse pursuing predators.

Their bills are long and slender, as long as their heads. The length and strength permit them to penetrate bark crevices for insects and open shells of nuts or acorns for the meat or grub within. This feeding habit is the source of their name.

Yank yank yank is a familiar woodland sound. It is surmised that their interpair calls, resembling a creaking tree, are another predator protection device.

No matter how raw the day, nuthatches join chickadees and titmice to troop winter woods seeking food. They are constant customers at bird feeders, particularly relishing black oil sunflower seeds. Fussily sorting on the bird tray, Whitey will pick up one seed after another before finding one to his liking. He may pick up fifteen or sixteen, scattering feed widely, before carrying the chosen one to a nearby tree. Inserting the seed into a bark crevice, he hammers out a kernel. Then a quick dash back to sort through again for a perfect one. What are his criteria? Weight? Color? Sometimes he doesn't pause to eat, just stows seeds in the bark as a handy pantry. Especially fond of beef suet, winter's equivalent of insect protein and fat, the bird tidily wipes its bill on a branch, first one side and then the other, after chipping at suet cakes.

Legs are short and thick compared to the dainty thin pins of companion chickadees. Long toes are strong, with a heavy hind toe and sharp, strongly curved claws. This combination enables him to descend headfirst down a tree trunk, defying gravity and finding insects and eggs unseen by climbers. Unlike woodpeckers and brown creepers, nuthatches do not use their stubby tails for support but rely on their claws to anchor them to the bark.

Red-breasted nuthatches are uncommon visitors, irrupting in some winters and never appearing in others. The winter of 1994 brought them south in record numbers.

These tiny birds dash in to a feeder, search out the perfect sunflower seed while scuttling around the platform, and take off in an instant. Within ten seconds they flash back for another seed and another and another.

Rather than eating them, they often bury them. Do they remember where they are when the snows are deep?

These birds, with distinct personality traits, are an inch shorter than their white-breasted cousins. They weigh less than a half ounce and sport a white eyebrow above a bandit-like black eye line. Their bills are shorter than their heads. Their blue is more intense than their cousins', and their cousins' red breast is really a warm rust. There is less white on the outer tail feathers than on white-breasted nuthatches. Again, females are grayer, noticeable because their crowns contrast less with the blue backs. Voice is one of Rosie's greatest charms, a miniature tin horn or oboe-like *toot toot* that carries a long distance.

Red-breasteds are often found in evergreen forests since they like the seeds which they deftly pry from cone scales. The birds glean branches and outer twigs of trees. I once saw one go the full length of a twenty-five foot limb, walking upside down along the bottom side, stopping periodically to eat a morsel. They consume beetles, wasps, caterpillars, and spruce budworm moths as well as dashing out for flying insects. Rosies often make aggressive jabs at larger birds on feeders.

December 16, 1993

Eastern Bluebird

What's your "I want to see it most of all" bird? A great gray owl? A black rail? For many people it's the eastern bluebird.

Bluebirds are closely related to robins and brown thrushes, but unlike them, they nest in holes rather than on branches. Originally, their favorite sites were cavities in dead tree limbs or trunks. Fuel shortages resulted in woods free of dead material. Also, when farmers discontinued fences or substituted metal posts, they eliminated another favorite nesting site—wooden posts. Bluebirds were scarce after heavy losses in the middle south during the long cold winters of the mid-1950s and '70s. Populations were also affected negatively by urban sprawl, house sparrow predation, and pesticide poisoning. The outlook for survival became gloomier and gloomier.

After the mid-fifties losses, a nationwide movement to construct trails of man-made nesting boxes gave the birds another chance; they responded dramatically. In addition to providing suitable houses, trained volunteers closely monitor them, removing house sparrow nests, discouraging wasp invasion and raccoon predation, and making repairs. Originally started in the 1920s and 30s, but de-emphasized during World War II, thousands of bluebird trails have been maintained throughout North America. One in Saskatchewan's prairies extends for 2,000 miles. Many birders, however, still think that bluebirds are hard to find.

Properly built houses help discourage house sparrows. Mounted not more than five feet above the ground, the entrance hole should be one and a half inches round with no front perch. A sheathed and greased pole and a double thickness of wood around the entrance hole make it hard for raccoons to reach in and destroy eggs or nestlings. Bluebirds prefer nest sites in open fields of low vegetation away from buildings, with scattered trees or shrubs for perching.

Bluebirds are not seed eaters and will not be seen at feeders. Look for them along country roads near pastures. Leisurely driving along park roads at Fort Custer, with its 150 bluebird houses, assures you of seeing them during the nesting season. Their mellow, gentle warble is not heard easily over automobile engine noise, so stop when you can and listen.

Adult males, about six inches long, have a bright blue back and head and a ruddy breast, throat, and sides. "The bluebird carries the sky on his back," said Henry David Thoreau. The female's similar pattern shows duller, more subdued colors. When a pair sits together in a treetop near the nestbox, one feels deeply grateful for such a beautiful and welcome sight. In certain lights, plumage appears black. Learn to recognize their rather dumpy silhouettes as they sit on telephone wires or a fence.

During March males take the initiative in nest site selection. It takes the female four to nine days to carry in and shape all materials with casual help from him. Using only uniformly sized, fine, dried soft grass, or even pine needles, a neat shallow nest cup with smooth flat edges is carefully woven. One lovely sky-blue egg is laid daily for four or five days, after which the female starts incubating them. She is tied there day and night for about two weeks, leaving only long enough to grab a little nourishment.

Young bluebirds are born naked, red, and bulgy. The male helps with the gargantuan task of feeding them for sixteen to twenty-three days at six- to eight-minute intervals. Severe weather may terminate first nestings. In such cases parents nest again, but usually not in the same box—another good reason for close monitoring so old nests can be discarded and boxes made available.

By the time nestlings are fully feathered and ready to fledge, sex differences in coloring are apparent. Their breasts are spotted as are other thrush family young. Adults constantly remove soft sacs of fecal material, keeping the nests immaculate. A vacated nest is so clean and neat that it's sometimes hard to tell if it has been used.

Nesting for a second brood starts immediately, absorbing all the female's energy. Males help the newly fledged first brood find food and shelter.

During a single nesting season, one box may shelter a variety of tenants. Last spring, for example, I opened one on May 6th to find a moss nest with a chickadee sitting on six eggs. On the 31st, I banded four nestlings. On June 8th this nest remained intact but empty. By the 19th, it had been stuffed with uniform small twigs and contained five cinnamon-spotted house wren eggs. This nest failed.

Then, success! On July 1st, a bluebird nest containing four warm, blue eggs was in place. The young were banded on the 26th. On checking the box again in August, hoping for a late second nesting, I found only a large number of wasps which I neither counted nor banded.

May 16, 1991

Cedar Waxwings

A cedar waxwing is one of the most pleasing of Michigan's birds. Always beautifully tailored, always sleek and neat, always demure and usually well-behaved, its only failing is a tendency to inebriation. When ripe berries have fermented, the bird overindulges and becomes tipsy. Gone is the correct posture and dignified manner. Forbush wrote of such an occasion in *Birds of Massachusetts*:

> Their actions were very comical, for they were helpless. One fellow bobbed up and down even after we had secured him under my hat...some tumbled to the ground where with outstretched wings they attempted to run away; still others tottered on the branches with wings continually flapping, as though for balance...they kept up a continual hissing noise, as a family of snakes might do.

The tidy, erectile crest and golden yellow band across the bottom of its tail are this bird's most notable field marks. When a large flock gathers quietly in a leafless tree, pale satiny yellow breasts and dark velvety smudges around eyes are apparent. Overall, the general impression is of silky fawn colorings. Sometimes wingtips contain a bright red wax-like substance visible only at close range. The function of those waxy droplets is unknown. Also, look for its white undertail coverts. If these feathers are bright red brown, then you have the larger and rarer Bohemian waxwing which frequently travels with unpredictable, wandering cedar waxwing flocks. This bird also has conspicuous white and yellow in its wing feathers, but undertail coverts are unmistakable. Isn't it nice to have a foolproof field mark?

Nesting in both upper and lower peninsulas, peak periods for seeing waxwings in southwest Michigan are from May 10th through June 10th and from September 20th through October 29th. They are especially noticeable before and after the nesting season when flocks gather and roam together in search of food. Thirty, forty, or fifty of these berry eaters will feed together in an area until hawthorn or high-bush cranberry bushes are picked clean. Then they move on together to fruitier pastures. Waxwings eat quantities of mountain ash, pokeberry, pyracantha, autumn olive, and mulberry fruit. They feed close together, making for good viewing by bird watchers. When fruit is plentiful, they may eat so much they can scarcely fly.

These birds have unlimited appetites for cankerworms, those little inch-long green worms which swing on invisible threads. Can you believe that a flock of thirty may eat 90,000 cankerworms in a month? They also seem to enjoy sugar maple's sweet sap when it is flowing. Many will fly over river or pond to catch flies in the manner of swallows or phoebes.

An engaging ritual occurs when birds line up on a branch and pass a cherry or caterpillar back and forth, from bird to bird, until someone in the row finally swallows it. A courting pair may exchange an insect or flower petal in similar fashion. Erratic flocks break up at June nesting time, and individuals go their own ways.

Loosely woven nests of twigs, grasses, and pine needles are built in a fork of almost any kind of tree, occasionally on a horizontal limb six to fifty feet above ground. I've watched their nests in a tamarack in a bog, in a small sumac in a dune area, and in a black oak at the edge of a parking lot. The attentive male feeds the female as she incubates pale gray eggs. Three to five young will leave the nest about fourteen to eighteen days after hatching. There are commonly two broods in a season. Occasionally, if they're short of nesting territory, waxwings nest colonially.

The most common sound of waxwings is a high-pitched, soft, thin lisp, a prolonged *see see*. An occasional husky call note may be heard.

It's always interesting to watch a flock of these debonair birds perched quietly together. Suddenly they all take off flying easily in an undulating course, much like a well-disciplined and graceful dance troupe or a flight of shore birds.

May 28, 1989

Who Hangs Around

What birds winter in southwestern Michigan? Who stays all year? Who comes down from the north to hunt for foods not available under harsher winter conditions or crop failures? Which are the most common winter residents, the rarest? What species are increasing or decreasing?

Some interesting and reliable answers to these questions became clearer to me while studying a statistical summary of Christmas bird counts in the Dowagiac area. These were performed under supervision of the Kalamazoo Nature Center and the Audubon Society of Kalamazoo. Residents of larger southwest Michigan communities might see more feeder-type birds whereas farm folk find more hawks and water birds. However, the total of 110 species in fifteen count years, made within eight days of Christmas, is representative of southwest Michigan.

Sadly, the top two most common birds are unwanted nonnatives, European starlings and house sparrows. Prolific breeders, these Eurasian birds were introduced into this country more than 100 years ago and have adapted all too well. Both species are year-round residents and compete with desirable native species for nesting sites. They do eat some insects that damage crops.

Starlings have heavily flecked plumage in winter, in contrast to black and greenish gloss feathers of spring. Their heavy yellow bills are unmistakable at any time. This species is found in almost all habitats, except forests, while dingy, streaked brown and black house sparrows are more common close to human habitations.

The third and fourth most common birds are winter visitors from the north: dark-eyed juncos and trim, handsome American tree sparrows. These shy species are seen from November to April, usually on or near the ground in brushy areas. Juncos may nest as far south as the Upper Peninsula, but tree sparrows breed only in arctic or subarctic areas.

In order of frequency, the remaining top ten are: crow, mourning dove, black-capped chickadee, American goldfinch, rock dove (another nonnative species), and blue jay. All were plentiful every year.

At the other end of the scale, birds recorded only once in fifteen years were: white-winged scoter, peregrine falcon, rusty blackbird, pine grosbeak, and white-winged crossbill, all from the far north. Pine grosbeaks and crossbills are irruptive winter migrants, showing here only rarely. There were also four summer residents that, for some reason, did not migrate: moorhen, house and marsh wrens, and gray catbird.

The stunning and gregarious evening grosbeak, another irregular migrant, was spotted in half of the years.

He moves from west to east, rather than from north to south. Charming common redpolls also appeared half of the time, typically in good numbers. The hoary redpoll was not observed on any counts. If he comes at all, it is in late winter when severe arctic cold finally drives him south.

Eastern bluebirds usually winter south of Michigan, but good food crops and mild December weather kept a few for two-thirds of the time. Purple finches, sometime local nesters, often appear in winter when large numbers withdraw from northern areas. They were on most tallies in modest numbers. House finches, who were not found in the early 1980s, show up regularly now as they become more at home.

To think that counters find 110 species in the Dowagiac region, albeit often in small numbers, is a testament to the structure and lifestyle of winged creatures. A feather seems such a frail thing to provide waterproof warmth and to make flight possible. With adequate food supplies, birds have amazing abilities to survive storms.

January 28, 1995

Audubon Christmas Bird Counts

"Jeepers, look at that. Fifty-nine horned larks and two snow buntings!" They were feeding avidly at the side of the highway in soft snow. It was so deep that only their backs showed as dark spots; their heads were buried, eating whatever it was. Was it road salt they were after? When a car passed, they flew to the cornfield but came right back. They were the best birds of this day in Allegan and brought our total number of species to thirty.

Audubon Christmas Bird Counts, now almost a century old, are a staple of American bird study. More than 40,000 people participate in 1,500 counts throughout North and Central America. Local groups designate circles fifteen miles in diameter and a specific twenty-four hour period. Dates, set by the National Audubon Society, are from late December to early January. A compiler organizes the event, assigns areas, and submits a final report, which is no small task.

Plans are carefully developed and teams sent to sites known to be productive. Some observers cover backyard feeders while watchers on foot and in cars peruse local woodlands, parks, beaches, waterways, cattle feeding stations, marshes, and ponds, tallying as they go. Even owls are lured and listed while it is still dark.

I remember a bitter December night in northern Indiana when my living room floor had bedrolls spread out stuffed with recumbent bodies of owl counters who vanished at four a.m. Large plates of homemade sweet rolls, bags of apples, and jugs of coffee vanished too. Playing cassette tapes of owl calls at known sites, observers located four species: great horned, barred, screech, and saw-whet. Later, duck observers saw a snowy owl on a Lake Michigan beach. Pure luck.

In Florida, I've helped spot beautiful long-legged waders and dozens of scurrying shorebirds at Ding Darling Sanctuary. Some of our team counted from canoes.

In Arizona, before sunup, we stopped at a certain tall palm tree where a barn owl was known to roost. We recorded handsome desert sparrows and thrashers and estimated 1,800 yellow-headed blackbirds on utility wires above a cattle feeding site. I'd never seen even one yellow-head before. That amazing sunrise view is an experience I shall long remember.

In Yellowknife, at the Canadian Arctic's edge, with the thermometer at a cool fifteen degrees below zero, a few hardy souls waited for Christmas day's ten a.m. sunrise. We counted all-black ravens and all-white ptarmigans, spruce grouse, boreal chickadees, and gray jays. Redpoll flocks moved so rapidly, looking for seeds on stunted birches, that we could only guess at numbers. We hoped for a gyrfalcon but none appeared. House sparrows, opportunists that they are, were seen only downtown flying from under one warm, newly parked car to another.

In Cass County, Michigan, we went out in darkness on December twentieth hoping to call in an owl. Christmas stars on silos and ridgepoles shone out cheerily through a dreary drizzle. Candle lights in farm house windows were a homey sight. A barred owl responded clearly to a tape, but the screech owl did not. Hearing an owl's voice always distresses small birds; they wish to drive this unseen enemy out of town. One black-capped chickadee was particularly agitated and perched on our side view mirror.

Cedar waxwings and common redpolls were in nice large flocks. An odd shaped stump at the edge of a stream turned into a bedraggled great blue heron, so hunched up against chill winds and swirling snow as to be unreal.

Kestrel, rough-legged, red-tailed, and one accipiter were our hawks for the day. Dropping temperatures, wet snow, and widespread fog made identification increasingly difficult but two eastern bluebirds appeared in one woods. They must survive on Michigan holly and highbush cranberry fruits. Blue jays fed actively on horse manure in the snowy road. No evening grosbeaks or crossbills appeared, our sometime winter treats.

Results of these counts depend on skills, knowledge, patience, and especially the day's weather. One year in the Indiana Dunes we had over 220 red-headed woodpeckers, the most of any tally in the country that year. Next year we didn't see any of them, or anything else, because we wakened to twenty-six inches of beautiful fluffy, white snow which had buried everything, even our snow shovels, overnight.

Christmas counts attract top field birders to high density areas such as Freeport, Texas, where camaraderie and good natured competition prevail. Results are published the following summer. Comparisons reveal a nationwide picture of the well-being, or otherwise, of our feathered friends.

November 26, 1994

Henderson

Of Petals

Barbellate or Glochidiate?
Or What is Texture?

One of my favorite botany texts, James P. Smith's *Vascular Plant Families*, has a page with twenty-six meticulously drawn diagrams of ways a plant can be hairy. A few terms are familiar, such as mealy or glandular, but most are new and strange.

With copied list in hand, it's fun to walk woodland paths searching for applications of such words. Many flower species have stems or leaves that are hairy in various degrees. In large genera like violets, species may be separated by the pubescence of various parts, especially beards on petals.

Backs of leaves emerging on silver poplar trees are thick with soft whiteness and are therefore tomentose or glabrate. As these parts mature, whiteness disappears and parts become glabrous, without hairs.

Sprawling halberd-leaved tearthumb of damp meadows is well named. Harsh retrorse (bent backward), strigose (sharp and stiff) prickles cover its stem.

Do you know the stately spikes of colic root with its soft green well-proportioned basal rosettes? The inside of white blossoms looks like the surface of a dish of farina (cream of wheat). Hence, colic root flowers are said to be farinose.

Lower stems of cinnamon fern stalks have tufts of cinnamon colored, loosely attached, soft hairs and are termed floccose.

If you're fortunate to find a *Boletes frostii* mushroom in a damp autumn woods, you'll note the stem is covered with unusual netlike lines and is reticulate. The dramatic top section of this six- to eight-inch circle appears to be a pie made of dragon's blood.

Hepatica plants emerging in early April are almost hidden by dense fuzzy white hairs. They are canescent.

Parts of prairie lead-plants are densely furry, so gray-hoary they give it a dull lead-like appearance. Prairie's silky aster is so-called because of long, silvery hairs covering both sides of the leaves, making it sericeous. Its bracts are pilose, covered with soft distinct hairs.

Wild gooseberry of beech-maple woods may have all parts, including the fruit, covered with sharp prickles and is spinescent.

If hairs are barbed at tips, as prickly pear cacti, they are glochidiate. These tiny, almost invisible hooked barbs are more annoying than the sharp spines. Ask anyone who's tried to remove a few hundred of them from a finger tip.

Of all hairy textures I've encountered, the sedge called cotton-grass is most memorable. Southwest Michigan bogs support a modestly flowered member of the genus, tawny cotton-grass. But in alpine and arctic regions, flower heads are larger than golf balls. Acres of otherwise starkly empty rocky expanses filled with waving plumes of silky white bristles make an indelible impression on the observer. Arctic natives braided cotton grass fibers for wicks in whale oil lamps.

Bull-thistles have extremes of harshness and softness. Stems and leaves are covered with hedgehog-like spiny, echinate prickles, but densely clustered lavender florets are an inviting lush fluffiness.

Biennial common mullein's thick wooly felted surfaces are velutinous, having velvety hairs protecting soft green tissue during winter months. Use a hand lens to observe that tiny hairs of the pubescence are all branched.

And so words go on. I've never met a malpighiaceous plant, with forked hairs attached at the middle, and I hope I never do.

September 24, 1992

Botany by Bicycle

If you like wildflowers, if you have a curiosity bump, and if you live in Kalamazoo County, you are fortunate to have a helpful book. Although no longer in print, it is available in many libraries.

In 1947, Clarence and Florence Hanes published *Flora of Kalamazoo County, Michigan.* The 295 pages were the result of many years of painstaking observations in the field followed by hours of study in botanical texts. After each field trip, collected plant specimens were meticulously prepared for pressing and drying. Their parts were arranged to show definitive characteristics as clearly as possible.

When the Depression hit in the early thirties, these former school teachers suffered heavy financial losses. Rather than sitting around grieving over worthless bank shares and nonexistent stock dividends, they wanted to do something that would keep them happily busy and be useful to others. They decided to make a collection of all plants growing within five miles of Schoolcraft.

Clarence was born in 1874 to Schoolcraft farmers and lived his entire life in the house in which he was born.

Florence, daughter of a school principal and botany teacher from Comstock and Alamo, was in her forties when they embarked on their ambitious project. A five-mile limit was necessary because their only mode of transportation was one well-used bicycle. Later, when an old truck was loaned them, they studied the entire county. Eventually, area botanists often joined them on collecting trips which turned into friendly picnics. When puzzling plants required expert help, the couple sought classification from professional botanists in museums and universities.

In addition to dozens of plant collecting expeditions, they made maple syrup for sale in late winter months and did all necessary chores requisite to running an orchard and small farm with gardens, cows, and chickens.

Clarence was a familiar sight riding through town, guiding his bike with one hand and swinging a pail of milk in the other. Friends remember him as a tall, slim figure characteristically wearing overalls and high rubber boots.

While both had the usual tenth grade botany course and Clarence had done some collecting around Schoolcraft, neither received serious training in plant classification. But they attacked the many problems seriously and with good will. He maintained interest in the local school board and Florence was treasurer of the Schoolcraft Ladies Library Association for thirty years.

From entries in a daily diary which Florence kept from 1937 to 1965, we learn that Clarence determined the species and pressed specimens while she mounted dried plants and prepared identifying labels, written in a fine Spencerian hand. We also learn they collected and identified 1,749 species and varieties, about fifty of them not previously recorded for Michigan. Attesting to the botanic richness of their home village, 1,340 types of plants were found within the initial five miles, including the "Island" just west of town, the Sugarloaf lakes, and their surrounding marshes and woodlands.

A storehouse of botanical knowledge, unique to this county, resulted from the Hanes' years of dedicated and painstaking work. Their herbarium plates are preserved in the Hanes Herbarium at Western Michigan University and their extensive correspondence at The University of Michigan at Ann Arbor, available to university scientists preparing *Flora of Michigan*.

Clarence passed away in 1956. Several years later Western Michigan gave Florence an honorary Doctor of Science degree. She wrote in her diary: "What a pity Clarence couldn't have shared in it." The Haneses are buried near an ancient sycamore tree in the Schoolcraft Cemetery. Their dark red granite gravestone is engraved with a graceful spray of flowering dogwood.

August 12, 1993

Cattails

The lowly cattail is well-known to everyone, nature lover or not. Sunny, marshy places dominated by these sword-like plants are a familiar sight across North America, in subarctic, temperate, and tropical climates.

Dense clusters grow in shallow water in permanently wet areas and may reach six to eight feet. Soft green leaves are long, narrow, flat, and spiky, D-shaped in cross section. They point upward to avoid shading and are sheathed at the base. Edges rather than blades are presented to an intense and glowing midday sun. Leaves usually rise above flower stalks. Their tough, pliable texture and pleasing soft color make them useful for constructing mats and chair seats. A waxy finish helps keep water from blocking breathing pores. The plants are unbranched and usually have eight or more leaves.

Tiny, yellowish male flowers, so small as to be indistinguishable, are densely packed on the upper part of a heavy spike. Brownish female flowers are massed lower on the same spike, just touching male flowers. When stamens drop their abundant powdery pollen on female pistils, they develop into the familiar thick, cylindrical brown sausage. Dried flower arrangers gather flower spikes by July fourth while they are attractively pencil-sized and not apt to disintegrate quickly. A good pruning shear and a strong arm are necessary for cutting heavy, fibrous stems.

Mature flower stalks protect minute seeds with masses of fine, silky hairs that aid in dispersal. Copious amounts of soft, white down help seeds become windborne. They also make for good fun fights in fall. Each sausage may have as many as one million seeds.

Broad-leaved cattails, the midwest's most common species, have no space between upper male flower areas and lower female parts, which become the cattail. Narrow-leaved ones, superficially similar, have distinct gaps between the two flower sets, slimmer cattails, and leaves less than a half inch wide. Common along the east coast, some botanists say this species tolerates salt and alkali waters better than the broad-leaved. The hardy broad-leaved moves into a roadside ditch, often invading within a year after a grading operation. The two species often hybridize.

Bulky plants multiply not only by an unbelievable number of seeds but also by spreading vegetatively via rhizomes. In spring, the main stem works its way through rich marsh muck and sends up new shoots. When it dies, each shoot becomes a new plant. In this way, a single seed colonizes a whole area in a few short years, whether the landowner wishes such an invasion or not. Getting rid of unwanted colonies is difficult. Burning may destroy seeds and masses of aboveground growth but, except in an unusually dry period, may not kill extensive root systems. If high water levels are maintained throughout summer, they may retard growth. Cutting the entire surface growth just before heads mature and mowing a month later when new growth is three to four feet high, may kill seventy five percent of the plants. Their density eliminates growth of aster, goldenrod, boneset, turtlehead, spotted Joe Pye weed, gentian, water plantain, blue iris, arrowhead, water-lily, pitcher-plant, grass of Parnassus, and other beautiful wetland flowers we all cherish.

Cattail marshes provide food and homes for certain birds and mammals. Red-winged blackbirds, the most obvious residents, suspend their loosely woven cup nests of dried leaves among strong erect stems. The male's carefree *konk la reee*, uttered from an old stalk, is conspicuous. Young red-wings clamber among sturdy plants before they can fly, providing lunch for lurking bullfrogs or snapping turtles.

Marsh wrens, too, are major inhabitants; brown, small, and reclusive as they are, their presence is more heard than seen. Rails and bitterns live in the deep cover but find cattail seeds too small and too hairy to be palatable. Ducks use the cover but prefer to feed in more open areas.

Muskrats inhabit these marshes in great numbers, building their familiar mud and stalk mounds and stockpiling down and shredded leaves in nests within. So great is their taste for the starchy underground stems, a family can reduce the plants' populations significantly.

Cattails were important in native Indian cultures.

Young shoots were eaten raw or cooked. Rootstocks were roasted or dried and pounded into flour. Porridge was made of the tiny seeds. Staminate pollen was gathered and used with flour. Masses of soft down were used in quilts and, like milkweed down, as diaper lining for papooses.

June 6, 1991

Dandelion

Emerson described a weed as a plant whose virtues haven't yet been discovered. Most of us think of a weed as a plant out of place, usually an alien invader, and a troublesome one which resists removal. It could be an orchid in a cranberry bog, but it's more apt to be dandelion in a lawn, sheep sorrel in a lettuce bed, thistle in a cornfield.

Every spring dandelion battles are enjoined again. Are you for or against them? Are you for strong sprays and a country club lawn? Or for letting Mother Nature have her way? She'll sprinkle your lawn for free with golden yellow blossoms. The soil will have no chemicals and be full of worms to nourish waiting, hungry robins.

Weeds share a number of traits that guarantee success: preference for disturbed ground, vigorous and rapid growth, and a high degree of fertility. Dandelions meet these criteria and have other persistent qualities. Not only do they thrive in sterile, disturbed fields and roadsides but also in established lawns and gardens. Spring flower and leaf buds are set the previous fall, ready to rise and shine vigorously the minute the sun becomes bright and warm. And in the realm of fertility, they get an A+ grade, with 150 to 200 ray flowers on every stem. To the dismay of those who want a pool table-like lawn, as Peterson describes it, a mower does little to discourage dandelions because leaf rosettes and flower buds lie flat on the ground. Dandelions defy hand weeding because the eight- to ten-inch long tough root is slippery, hard to grasp and withdraw. If you don't get all of it, you soon may have another plant.

A native of Eurasia, one of twenty-five *Taraxacum* species in the world, our dandelion received its common name from early botanists who gave it a French one, dent de lion, for they thought the jagged, toothed leaves resembled lions' teeth. We corrupted this to dandelion. The bright flower now is found throughout temperate climates, with greatest abundance in the eastern United States. Interestingly, it is not found in many arctic areas because tundra soils lack nitrogen. But where human settlements, animal dens, or bird cliffs are located, nitrogen is available and dandelions flourish.

These plants alternately have been honored and cursed as far back as the first Passover when it was one of the bitter herbs. Ancient Egyptians reportedly used it to relieve stomach aches. American folklore claims it as an internal medicine and diuretic. Roots were dried and ground as a coffee substitute. The bitter milky juice in flower stems has been used to treat warts.

Seed-eating birds enjoy the tiny seeds, particularly house sparrows and American goldfinches. The latter may get as much as two to five percent of their food from the plant, partly because it flowers and sets seed over such a long period. The pocket gopher of Utah eats the seeds and foliage to obtain half its total food intake.

Delicate little parachute plumes cling to every finely ribbed seed, increasing the efficiency of wind dispersal. Every child knows how important it is to help the wind along. An 1899 wildflower book said of the fluffy seed ball: "...the children blow it to tell what o'clock it is. There are usually four good blows in a ball of down and this fact has won for it the name of 'four o'clock', each blow signifying an hour."

A pleasant memory involving children occurred years ago when driving out of the city on a bright spring day. As we passed a forest preserve sheeted with golden dandelions, a usually shy three-year-old lass in the car said, "I need to pick those flowers." Not "May I?" or "Could we?" but "I need." A true flower lover.

Many people have sampled dandelion leaves in salads or eaten a few lightly braised at some time or other. Today on the east coast, these gourmet salad greens sell for as much as $1.25 a pound. Vineland, New Jersey, is the center of this greenhouse culture. Proponents claim that the greens have as much iron as spinach, more potassium than bananas, and fifty percent more Vitamin C than tomatoes. Leaves picked before the flowers appear are less acid than when they are older and taste much like endive. Some growers in Europe even blanch them. Dandelion wine is a tasty country brew made from its flower petals, oranges, lemons, sugar, and yeast.

Taraxacum is of Persian origin and *officinalis* refers to the fact that dandelions are used by pharmacists. As recently as 1940, more than 100,000 pounds of roots were imported for use in tonics and liver medicines. If there is such a thing as a virtuous weed, the dandelion may be one.

April 25, 1991

Orchids

Kalamazoo County has the distinction of having the longest list of threatened species of any county in Michigan. Why do we have such a record? One reason may be the exhaustive botanizing of the 576 square-mile county conducted by the Haneses in the 1930s and '40s.

This area also boasts a diversity of habitats supporting all kinds of flowers. There are river valleys, prairie remnants, bogs and marly fens, lots of lakes and woods, and especially beech-maple woods. Forest and prairie soils consist of twenty-nine different classifications. As a result, many plant families are represented. Among them are a few remnants of the popular orchid family, flowers of irresistible beauty. Due to their showy loveliness, native orchids are hanging on precariously. Over the years, thoughtless or unknowing people and commercial exploiters either picked or tried to transplant them, not realizing that invisible mycorrhizal fungi in the soil are absolutely essential to their existence. Without this fungus, infinitely small seeds cannot germinate and roots cannot grow. Deer are exceedingly fond of tender orchid leaves and have destroyed many colonies.

Blossoming in boggy or sandy areas in May, is pink lady-slipper or moccasin-flower. *Cypripedium acaule* has a pair of large, hairy basal leaves with prominent parallel veins. The single flower, the moccasin, a sac-like lip, is pink with darker pink veins. Cleft down the front, it is a unique shape. It still flowers in profusion in favored sites. Edward Voss, in *Michigan Flora*, maps these flowers for fifty-one of sixty-five counties in the Lower Peninsula.

The scientific name of showy lady's-slipper, *Cypripedium reginae*, is indeed descriptive of its queenly, regal beauty. Largest of our orchids, the stalks grow to twenty inches and bear two or three stunning terminal pink and white slippers. This plant in full bud, just as petals spread to reveal the lip, is unbelievably exquisite in shape and pastel shading.

Threatened *Cypripedium candidum* hides its charming dainty and fragrant white lady's-slippers amid grasses and sedges in moist calcareous soils. Intolerant of heavy shade and of any disturbance such as grazing or plowing, it is a rare find within its limited range. Golden Alexanders and shrubby cinquefoil often grow nearby.

The *Liparis* genus contributes Loesel's twayblade, also called fen orchis or bog twayblade, to our wetlands. Its two to eight inches are easily overlooked among grasses and tamarack trees. Stalks bear eight or ten yellowish-green flowers, each about one-quarter inch long. Yellow seed pouches are often more noticeable than blossoms.

Orchids have a complicated pollination system, but when it's successful as many as a million infinitely small seeds develop. Germination, too, is difficult and plants may be eight to ten years old before they flower. Let us all look at orchids long and appreciatively and let them be.

If you're interested in learning about them, there are several useful reference books. Fred Case of Saginaw, who has spent much of his life studying orchids, produced an update of his excellent *Orchids of the Great Lakes Region* in 1987. In 1993, the Indiana Academy of Sciences published Michael Homoya's *Orchids of Indiana*, a superb volume both scientifically and aesthetically. The photographs are stunning. Maps cover the range of all species, including those found in Michigan.

July 28, 1994

Pokeweed

Pokeweed, or poke, is a bushy native plant of weedy tendencies which always intrigues me. It grows luxuriantly from enormous perennial roots, is in flower almost all summer, and produces quantities of attractive, juicy, purplish berries. What more can one ask of a plant?

Autumn hikers often stop to admire handsome clusters of rich, dark berries. If you have room on your property to entertain this large plant, by all means do so for birds' breakfasts and dinners. A copse with its thousands of berries is a great favorite of thrushes as well as flickers, especially during fall migration.

The plant is found in fields and woods, often in mildly or recently disturbed areas. Left alone, it develops thickets ten to twelve feet in diameter. Flowers and mature seeds are often present on racemes at the same time, an uncommon arrangement. Long-stemmed, smooth-edged leaves are large, thin, and conspicuously veined. Stem exteriors are tough and fibrous but interiors are honeycombed, pithy looking, and feel like a dried sponge.

Although it is included in the Peterson series *Edible*

Wild Plants field guide as a tasty spring green, instructions are filled with cautions. "Warning: Root, seeds, and mature stems and leaves dangerously poisonous. Be very careful not to include part of the root when collecting the shoots, and peel or discard any shoots tinged with red." The *American Medical Association Handbook of Poisonous and Injurious Plants* states: "Intoxication generally arises from eating uncooked leaves in salads or mistaking the roots for parsnips or horseradish. The toxin is phytolaccatoxin and related to triterpenes." The resulting forty-eight hour digestive upsets are unpleasant but usually not fatal.

Young shoots have large glossy leaves and are considered edible until they attain six inches. Boiled with two changes of water, some say they are as tasty as asparagus. Poke is especially popular in the South. I met a couple at an Audubon camp out who were so fond of the plant they grew half an acre of it.

Drooping racemes of blue-black berries grow on bright red stems. When treated properly, they produce a nonfast color dye giving the plant another of its common names: inkberry. Berries can also be used for pie filling. An 1893 wildflower book speaks of pokeweed having a reputation as a rheumatism remedy; in Pennsylvania, berries were mixed with whiskey to make port. Several texts mention the plant's unpleasant odor but I have not noticed this particularly.

Poke's long history as a native plant results in a large number of folk names: crowberry, pigeon-berry, skoke, pocan bush, cocum or cokan, and garget.

Helen V. Smith's *Michigan Wildflowers* informs us: "The Indians prepared a dull red or magenta pigment from the dried and pulverized berries and used it for stamping designs on baskets, using dies cut from potatoes."

Once established, this plant is hard to eradicate or transplant due to its massive root. Close inspection of its flowers reveals that they have no petals. Five white or pinkish petallike sepals surround ten pistils united into a ring, a unique arrangement. Berries, which may last through the winter, are perfect tiny rosettes resembling fancy buttons. Take one disc apart to find hard shiny black seeds, each about the size of a pinhead.

Phytolacca americana comes from Greek and French and refers to the crimson juice of unripened berries. It belongs to a family of twenty-two genera: herbs, shrubs, trees, and vines, most of which are tropical.

Eminent nineteenth century naturalist John Burroughs wrote of pokeweed: "What a lusty, regal plant it is! It never invades cultivated fields but hovers about the borders and looks over the fences like a painted Indian sachem."

July 22, 1993

97

Lobelias

Two of the loveliest late summer gems are cousins, members of the lobelia clan: cardinal-flower and great blue lobelia.

Linneaus named the genus in honor of Matthias de L'Obel, a sixteenth century Flemish botanist and author who served as physician to James I. It is thought that early French Canadians, enamored of these stunning red blossoms, sent specimens to Europe where their color was like robes of princes of the church. The name cardinal-flower was given.

Vivid crimson spikes of scarlet flowers shine brilliantly in shady swamps. One memorable day I found a sturdy six-foot spike with seventy-five showy blossoms growing among forty-odd flowering stems of normal size. It usually grows from two to four feet high. White forms of cardinal-flower are rare.

In addition to its glowing color, the texture and form of the two-inch blossom are dramatic. I've been reading botany texts for a long time, but only recently have I found any exclamation points. Famed Harvard botanist Asa Gray published *How Plants Grow* in 1880. The second half of the text is a series of plant descriptions intended for high school use. Of cardinal-flower he wrote: "Corolla unequally five-lobed, and split down to the bottom on the upper side! Stamens five, united into a tube both by their filaments and their anthers!" Use of exclamation points conveys the true drama of this flower. When stamens are pollinating, bits of pure white pollen drift down to the red velvet cushion below.

A perennial, it is a plant of shady low areas found at edges of swamps and streams. It multiplies by perennial offshoots, accounting for its colonial nature. Removing flower stalks before seeds form makes plants produce extra offshoots.

Hummingbirds feed hovering on the wing. The basal tube of the corolla enables their long straw-like tongue to reach nectar. Blossoms lack solid petal platforms that insects require for landing. Flowers on the stalk tend to be one-sided. Leaves are oblong or oval, thin, faintly pubescent, and pointed at both ends.

In August, 1842, Nathaniel Hawthorne wrote of this beauty: "For the last two or three days, I have seen scattered stalks of the cardinal-flower, the gorgeous scarlet of which it is a joy even to remember. The world is made brighter by flowers of such a hue."

The cardinal-flower is on Michigan's do not pick list..

Another striking flower of this genus, which numbers more than 380 members, is the great blue lobelia. The scientific name, *Lobelia siphilitica*, was given long ago when Europeans thought its roots could be used to treat syphilis. The treatment was not successful but the name stayed.

The one-inch blue blossom is tubular with two lips. There are two erect upper lobes, and the lower spreading three make a landing platform for insects. Rarely all white, the petals are striped with white. Like cardinalflower, five stamens are in a single ring around the pistil which projects upward through a slit in the upper lip. Investigate with a hand lens to see this unique arrangement.

Leafy stems grow on swamp edges, in damp woods, or in gardens. Spring foliage is attractive, a soft green rosette of closely nested leaves. Leaves are alternate, irregularly toothed, and stalkless, and grow progressively smaller up the stem. Great blue lobelia blossoms later than cardinal-flower, often lasting into October.

The *AMA Handbook of Poisonous and Injurious Plants* lists all parts of all members of the genus as poisonous, but "poisoning is uncommon except when plants are employed in home medicine...The dry plant material has little alkaloid activity...Lobeline was once used as a central nervous system stimulant in the treatment of respiratory depression and as an emetic." So mild is poisoning that lobelias are not included in the Kalamazoo Poison Prevention Council's brochure.

Watch a bumblebee as it leisurely feeds on great blue lobelia. This blue-loving insect cruises from blossom to blossom, sometimes not stopping but moving right on. Can it smell nectar? Does it take all the nectar in a single flower or leave some? Can plants replace nectar after the bee's visit?

August 6, 1992

The Gentian Family

Do you suffer from backache? American Indians did. To relieve this pain, they concocted a bitter drink from roots of gentian plants. And long, long ago, on the east coast of the Adriatic Sea, Gentius, King of Illyria, was perhaps the first to discover medicinal values of some gentians. He used the root infusion as an emetic, cathartic, and tonic drug.

Scientists place plants in families according to similarities in microscopic parts of their reproductive systems. Such sorting often makes for strange bedfellows, as viewed by untrained eyes. The family has seventy genera and 1,000 species, whose flowers vary from tiny, leafless screwstems to seven-foot, leafy American columbos.

The minute screwstem, a plant of damp and boggy areas, has opposite scale-like yellow-green leaves on wiry stems. Its flowers vary from white to purple or yellow. The dramatically tall *Swertia* or American columbo, of dry oak woods, is a leafy-stemmed plant with all parts arranged in fours. It blossoms erratically, but if you're lucky, you'll see yellowish petals dotted with brown or purple specks. Both plants are so rare they are not included in most field guides. The Haneses, however, found them in several Kalamazoo County sites.

The most familiar members are, of course, the gentian species. You may choose among fringed, lesser fringed, closed, downy, stiff, or yellowish species, each found in its own special habitat. In the old days, you also could choose my favorite, a stunning prairie species, soapwort gentian. But, sadly, that flower no longer is found in Michigan. The remaining gentians are protected in the state.

Fringed gentian with its intense coloring, graceful architectural shapes, and delicate deep fringe, is often called America's favorite wildflower. Number one or not, it is beautiful. Usually a biennial, it opens its treasures only to bright sun, foiling many a would-be photographer hampered by clouds on a day in the country. To find a two-foot tall plant with several dozen flaring, misty-blue blossoms is to be given a blessing.

Closed gentian, a perennial, doesn't open its richly blue petals to reveal white petticoats at all, either to sun or to shade. But it's fun to watch a bumblebee, the only insect strong enough to separate petals, force its way into blossom after blossom. These plants flower the latest of all; their petals often show lingering color as late as Christmas.

The small spur gentian is an inconspicuous plant with long-spurred, small, greenish blossoms. It is more common farther north in Michigan.

Rose-pink and showy centaury are two other midwest species. Rose-pink has a green, star-shaped center and is breathtaking in its loveliness. Winged stems and bright blossoms are found in moist soil or damp sand. The tiny showy centaury, introduced from Europe, decorates waste places with abundant, minute, bright pink blossoms.

Wildflower lovers familiar with alpine species rave, and rightly so, about gentians of high, dry, cold circumboreal areas. The plants may be small, but their large flowers are like vases and of an extraordinary intensity of blue. I remember my delight in finding an alpine gentian in a high meadow at Yosemite National Park one midsummer day. Swiss, German, and Austrian fans work hard to protect their many rare and stunning species, especially from those who would use them to flavor their aperitifs.

One visible feature common to all family members, regardless of genus or exact shade of blue, is opposite, stemless leaves. Watch for, enjoy, and protect these delightful plants. Do not pick them. Let them go to seed.

August 21, 1988

Autumn Wildflowers

Autumn wildflowers bring us a joyful array of yellows and lavenders, sprinkled here and there with white. Railroad embankments and blessedly unmowed roadsides glow with composites of every variety.

All too many of the 150 or more daisy species are look-alikes. Ditches and low damp places come into their own with wingstem, spotted Joe Pye weed, and giant ragweed vying for top honors. They bury turtlehead, hardhack, and even common evening-primrose in their height contest.

Sorting out goldenrods is the bane of botanists because species characteristics are often subtle and intergradings numerous. It could be a full-time occupation, and, if you're like I am, niceties of the differences would be forgotten all too soon. Each type of habitat seems to have its own species.

Showy goldenrod has a stout, reddish stem and smooth leaves. Its floral show peaked in August with lovely cylindrical plumes scattered through woods and open places. It's not as tall as some of its relatives, but makes up for that lack with showy flower and seed plumes.

In wet areas, watch for rough-leaved goldenrod growing to seven feet in height. It has large lower leaves, up to twelve inches, and a four-angled stem. Upper sides of leaves are harsh and rough but lower surfaces are smooth and veiny. Flowers are not distinctive, just a lot of lovely rods of gold.

Widely found grass-leaved goldenrod, also called flat-topped goldenrod, has slender leaves with smooth edges and usually three to five parallel veins. A hardy plant with broad tastes, it survives drought, carbon monoxide, and foot traffic. Other flat-topped goldenrods illustrated in Roger Tory Peterson and Margaret McKenny's *A Field Guide to Wildflowers* do not commonly occur in southwest Michigan. If you see one that is distinctively flattopped with center flowers opening first, it should be this species.

Blue-stem goldenrod is a late-blossomer which prefers rich woods and shady places. Its flowers appear along bluish stems in leaf axils instead of sending out rods. Note that the waxy bloom on the stem can be rubbed off easily.

Take any one of these minute blossoms apart with a scalpel. See if you can find both ray and disc flowers.

Don't make the old mistake of thinking goldenrods cause hay fever. If you observe for a while, you'll see they're insect pollinated, not by wind, and therefore couldn't irritate eyes and noses. Both common and giant ragweeds are waving inconspicuous flower spikes in September breezes and spell doom to hay fever sufferers. It's good to learn these two plants and to keep your property free of them. Above all, destroy the seeds.

Acres of wild cucumber vines grow along the Paw Paw River near Benton Harbor where they associate with red maple, speckled alder, buttonbush, red osier dogwood, and great water dock. One vine climbed twenty-five feet straight up in a big juniper. One of my favorite nature pleasures is to pick a two-inch fruit when it is dry and carefully remove bits of outer skin. Underneath I find a reticulated tissue of incredibly fine spun gold. When seeds are really dry, there are two openings in the top. Shake it a little and out pop large flat black seeds. Plant them in a damp sunny place next spring and grow your own vines.

Which autumn flower is fairest in your eyes?

October 8, 1994

Winter Evergreen Groundcovers

One joy of wandering winter woods is to find a bit of vegetation that still is truly green peeking through a spot bare of ice and snow. Richly endowed with evergreen trees, pines, spruces, yews, and hemlocks, southwest Michigan's winter snow cover often hides small herbaceous plants whose photosynthesis never seems to take a vacation.

Little evergreen plants learned to adapt to winter and a lack of available water. Woody stems and small leaves with waxy coatings help prevent evaporation. Many stems and leaves have hairy surfaces, another protective device. By keeping growth close to the ground, they benefit by being covered and out of desiccating winds. Because short summers limit seed production, most of these plants depend on vegetative reproduction. Trailing stems that root at nodes often form small colonies.

Where brooks run free all winter, watercress stays luxuriantly green. It is the same plant one finds in bunches at markets, often for a fancy price. If you can be sure the water source is free of pollution, a watercress sandwich made with seven grain bread and sweet butter is a gourmet reward for your harvesting efforts.

Caught among cress leaves and in many an eddy or quiet corner are hundreds, even thousands, of duckweed, the world's smallest flowering plant with the widest geographical distribution. With a leaf no bigger around than the eraser on your pencil, it has an unbranched root like a tiny hair and, on occasion, an even tinier flower. I've never yet been able to spot one in blossom, despite many efforts.

Away from moving water where it's colder, the growing condition is more hostile and plants must be sturdier. The familiar and popular Christmas fern is a handsome evergreen survivor scattered on shady hillsides in beech-maple woods. As winter progresses, stems weaken and lie prostrate. Long, narrow fronds keep their highly polished deep green look all winter. Pioneers used them for holiday decorations, hence their name. If you pry down in the humus a little way, you'll find next year's fronds curled tight and densely covered with protective brown scales.

Ebony spleenwort ferns, common in some woods, are notable for their relatively small size and shining black stalks.

Sensitive fern's fronds died back at first frost, thus its name. In damp places where it thrived, dying leaves left behind their hard, stiff fertile fronds, brown and dry, looking like strings of little beads. On close examination of each round bead, you can see openings where spores escaped. This abundant plant colonizes in low places in woods or on roadsides.

Club mosses are an old life form which once grew to

heights of a hundred feet or more. Now we call those compressed plants coal and use them as a heating fuel. Modern forms are found as groundcovers in protected woods. They are uncommon, but, if present at all, are frequently in large colonies. Their reproductive processes are much like ferns. Spores are released in such abundance that they were formerly gathered for fireworks or flash powder for cameras. When ignited, they produce a small explosive flash quite unexpectedly. Ground cedar, ground pine, shining club moss, and trailing club moss range from rare to infrequent in woods and around swamp edges.

The heath family contains the largest number of small evergreen plants, all of which adapted long ago to the rigors of winter. One heath member is partridgeberry. Characterized by a delicate, trailing habit, tiny opposite leaves have white mid-veins. Late spring brings small white trumpet flowers elegantly lined with white hairs. Flowers are always in pairs, two blossoms to one fruit, joined like Siamese twins. Bright red berries, ripening in fall, clearly show where the two flowers were attached. Game birds, foxes, even skunks, eat these berries with relish.

Bearberry, or Kinnikinnick as Indians called it, is a circumboreal evergreen groundcover of sandy areas, growing close to the southern edge of its range. The Haneses noted that it was rare "inland in Michigan south of Latitude 43°." They found it near Austin Lake. Where undisturbed, this creeping shrub often forms mats fifteen or twenty feet in diameter. In May, tiny pink dangling bell flowers of this dwarf shrub have great charm. Indians smoked its dried leaves.

Wintergreen, called checkerberry or teaberry, is an aromatic ground cover which grows luxuriantly in the north, but is found in suitable, undisturbed habitats of the lower peninsula. Short shoots are leafy at the top and bear small white bells. Tasty red berries hide in its foliage. Oil of wintergreen, formerly distilled from this plant, is now made chemically.

Trailing arbutus, or mayflower, is a rare jewel of Michigan's flora. A ground cover too, it grows in shade in sandy oak woods, raising its pale pink trumpet flowers of delightful fragrance in very early spring. It is really a shrub, although we generally think of it as a flower. Large, leathery oval leaves, still green, often have rusty spots by the end of January. They are replaced with new ones as soon as the flowers die. The stem is brown and hairy. Ants have a reputation of spreading arbutus seeds, which are as fine as dust. It is a rare plant in the Kalamazoo area but can be found at Grand Mere woodland.

Two additional small plants complete our woodland census. *Chimaphilas* of the pyrola family are well-known to those who love early spring wildflowers. Prince's pine, or pipsissewa, and spotted wintergreen prefer dry forest floor in oak-hickory woods, often in sandy soil. Both have small, waxy, nodding pink flowers. When I saw them the first time in the Great Smoky Mountains many, many years ago, I couldn't imagine any flower being so charming. Shiny, toothed leaves are whorled around the stem.

Bogs and swamps shelter evergreen plants. Heath

family's tiny cranberry and the buttercup family's lovely goldthread are found in wet birch-tamarack woods. Leatherleaf shrubs, one to three feet tall, another heath plant, are found near cranberry. Bishop Bog, west of Westnedge Avenue, has acres and acres of leatherleaf not just bordering a bog as it usually does. Deer and grouse enjoy their seeds.

Myrtle or periwinkle, a nonnative evergreen plant, is often found in the wild. It escaped from cultivation and has established large colonies in many places.

January 29, 1991

Henderson

Of Trees

First Blush

One of the natural world's fine spring displays is the flowers on trees. Where are they? Often up too high to be easy to enjoy. But their colors and component parts are so delicate and variegated that they are well worth pursuing. Some open, shed their pollen, and fade before leaves emerge. Wind pollination is uncertain at best; leaves would only block movement of tiny pollen grains.

Well-loved pussy willow, the earliest shrub to flower in southwest Michigan, thrives in marshes and swamps. Its familiar staminate catkins are soft and silvery-silky, turning golden yellow when pollen masses develop. Similar but inconspicuous greenish female flowers are borne on separate plants. Elliptical leaves are light green above and somewhat silky-hairy on the underside.

Doggerel from my childhood ran:

> Pussy Willow said "Meow
> Wish someone would tell me how
> Other kittens run and play
> Roll and frolic all the day."

Crimson and gold buds and tiny flowers of red maple trees are too small and too high in the air for casual observers to enjoy. Wind pollination's hit-or-miss process requires a great number of flowers in order to assure fertilization. This abundance occurs before leaves unfold, spreading a conspicuous red haze against cool blue spring skies. Ruby colored stamens comprise the male flower, and pistillate flowers are a contrasting golden color. A faint fragrance and enough nectar attract early bees which, thus, help the wind pollinate. Flower petals of both sexes are so small they escape notice. The familiar dangling V-shaped pairs of winged seeds drop by late May and germinate immediately. Red maples were always the first weeds in my vegetable garden every spring.

Box elder, or ash-leaved maple, opens its flowers before or with its leaves. Handsome drooping clusters of fringy pink male flowers appear on trees separate from those bearing little green female flowers. Fruiting abundantly, long ragged clusters of narrow-winged seeds hang through winter, unless it's a year for visiting evening grosbeaks who quickly dispose of these nutritious seeds.

Serviceberry goes by many names: sarvisberry, Juneberry, shadblow, or just plain shad. But all refer to various species and varieties of the genus *Amelanchier* and are beloved by spring woods walkers. They flower when the outdoors is still brown and dreary. It warms the heart to find delicate wispy white petals scattered over prevailing bleakness. Buds are daintily downy. Five strap-shaped petals are about an inch long, and there are five or six dangling blossoms on one raceme. Leaves, which unfold later, are downy at first. Shad is a popular tree with homemakers. It is hardy in southern Michigan, adapts to all soils, blossoms profusely, and bears tasty fruit enjoyed by humans and our feathered friends alike.

Prickly ash, a medium-sized shrub, is not a true ash, but it is prickly with scattered sharp, woody spines. Its scientific name, *Xanthoxylem americanum*, means yellow wood found in America. Red buds open into small yellow-green, lemon scented flowers which appear before the leaves. Butterfly larvae of giant and spicebush swallowtails feed on the leaves. Fruit capsules are bright red with two lustrous black seeds. The Haneses wrote that this shrub forms impenetrable thickets in upland and lowland woods.

If you find some of these early spring tree flowers which often go unnoticed, study their amazing details under a hand lens. This unimagined world of complexity and beauty is well portrayed by Walter Rogers in his book, *Tree Flowers of Forest, Park and Street.*

April 9, 1992

116

Spring Tree Flowers

Early flowering plum, pear, and cherry trees, both wild and cultivated, turn southwest Michigan into a flowery bower for weeks. White to pale pink blossoms open before leaves, making *Prunus* and *Pyrus* members the showiest of our blossom festival. As millions of buds open, orchards are transformed into fairylands.

Flowers are similar, with five petals, often on red stems. They open flat to display fifteen to twenty stamens to attract bees whose activities make pollination possible. So these insects are not eliminated, spraying for diseases must be done carefully .

Flowering apricot was imported from western Asia in the late nineteenth century. A hardy small tree, to thirty feet, it bears single whitish flowers in late April before the leaves emerge. Deep pink buds hug the ends of branches. Opened, they strongly resemble apple blossoms except their stamens are dark tipped. For proper pollination a few trees, not just one or two, are needed. Distinctive leaves are broad and rounded compared to plum and cherry leaves. Apricot trees are grown widely for their delicious fruit.

Sugar maples open their flowers in dangling clusters on hairy threadlike stalks, so numerous as to bathe tree tops in a yellowish haze. Winter buds are tinged with purple. Flowers appear in late April after leaves unfold, but seeds are not shed until late autumn.

White oaks are one of Michigan's largest and most valuable trees. When seen up close, their tiny staminate flowers are fairly attractive, with purplish-brown and yellow details.

Arranged along drooping, hairy catkin strands, these pesky masses later clog roof gutters and litter sidewalks and driveways. Lacking petals, it's hard to think of these blossoms as true flowers, but essential parts are present for reproduction. Male flowers outnumber the females by hundreds to one in order to assure adequate amounts of pollen. Borne separately on the same tree, small, furry female blossoms are reddish with red stigmas; if the wind graciously brings pollen from male neighbors, they will become acorns by fall. In contrast to most oak species, this acorn is ripe by its first autumn instead of the usual second season. Deep-capped acorns are sweet and tender, a favorite food of wood ducks, lesser prairie chickens, wild turkeys, jays, woodpeckers, bears, raccoons, squirrels, and deer.

Norway maples did come to us from Norway by way of England. Their well-shaped crowns, attractive foliage, and ability to survive city conditions made them popular as street and park trees, despite weedy proclivities. When their lovely clusters of flowers are in blossom, a hum of bees is noticeable some yards away. Male and female parts are on separate flowers but are similar in size, form, and color: five sepals, five cream or light yellow petals, and eight erect stamens. Wings holding long-stalked seeds are almost at right angles. These samaras spin down in autumn and germinate the next spring.

Pawpaw trees are common in woodland understories. They especially like moist, fertile bottomland soil. An inconspicuous, peculiar flower comes in late May just before the leaves. Three sepals and six overlapping petals of a purplish-brown or wine-red color are shaped in a little cup. Flowers have many stamens and short, stout hairy stems. Leaves are thin, broad, and may be as much as twelve inches long, a distinctive mark when you're woods walking. Caterpillars of zebra swallowtails feed on the foliage. Two- to five-inch long pulpy fruits, ripe in September, have an unusual flavor and contain several large flat seeds. Some people call them Michigan bananas. Leaves and fruit are aromatic or odorous, depending on your taste. Opinion about their edibility is strongly divided.

Flowering dogwood blossoms are perhaps the most familiar of all tree flowers. The tree's range is wide, its flowers lovely, and its fruits decorative and well-loved by birds. A small understory tree, it is usually not over twenty feet tall. During its blossom time, its beauty is everywhere. In the center of four ever-so-white bracts, the true flowers are tiny balls which turn into bright red berries in August and September. Dogwood arranges its branches in wide flat layers, displaying its floral array to best advantage.

April 23, 1992

Later Blossoms

Showy white flowers of European horse-chestnut trees come in June after leaves unfold. They are large and abundant, borne in handsome upright ten- to twelve-inch panicles that resemble pyramids. Throats of the five-lobed, bell-shaped, ruffled blossoms are spotted with yellow and red. Seven threadlike curving stamens protrude, adding to its dainty appearance. In autumn, large prickly husked capsules split into three pieces and release smooth brown seeds well-loved by children.

Basswood, or American linden, a stately shade tree sometimes surrounded by a circle of shoots, has lustrous winter buds in little red balls which develop into attractive heart-shaped, lopsided leaves. They flower in late June after leaves emerge. Fragrant, creamy white blossoms are in loose, drooping clusters with both male and female parts in a single half-inch flower. Sepals are small and look like five extra petals. Pistils are almost lost among stamens but develop into woody nutlets attached to long leafy bracts. These act as parachutes when seeds are ready to drop. Basswood nectar is a favorite of bees, and honey from it is considered unexcelled in flavor.

In late June, after the large heart-shaped leaves are fully grown, catalpa trees send out their cream colored blossoms. Deep bell-shaped flowers suggest small orchids in their daintiness. The prominent yellow and purplish spots and lines are lures to attract insects. Borne on purplish stems, the flaring flowers have ruffled edges on their five lobes. Identification of a close-up photograph of a single flower will puzzle all but the most knowledgeable of flower lovers, so striking is its beauty. Not native to Michigan, the catalpa was widely planted as an ornamental and became naturalized in cities and suburbs, becoming almost weedy in low places.

Staghorn sumacs are common in woods, thickets, or along roadsides. Their bark is a staple winter food for cottontail rabbits. Small, fragrant whitish-green flowers appear in conspicuous cone shapes in June and July. By September, velvety maroon female clusters bear hairy, acid seeds. If they are not used by children to make Indian lemonade, they stay all winter providing emergency food for birds, especially for invading evening grosbeaks which dote on them. This shrub is named for its velvety antler-like branches. Its intense scarlet leaves are one beauty of autumn roadsides. Often found in dense thickets, sumac sprouts freely when roots or trunks are disturbed.

Buttonbush, a tall shrub found in clones throughout boggy borders of wetlands, is easy to identify. Although its leaves, small and oval, resemble many other shrubs, its abundant flowers and seeds are unmistakable. Ping-Pong ball-size heads of 100 to 200 creamy white flowers which develop in midsummer are unique. All the little globes mature at the same time: perfect, delicate orbs. A dainty pistil protrudes from each and every tubular corolla. These fragrant flowers are attractive to butterflies, especially the painted lady. Small fruits remain in tight reddish balls, often through winter.

May 14, 1992

Northern White Cedar

Northern white cedar, or arbor vitae, was named *Thuja occidentalis* by Linnaeus. *Thuja* is Greek for a highly prized aromatic wood and *occidentalis* means western. The name arbor vitae originated with Frenchmen in Jacques Cartier's St. Lawrence River expedition who were stricken with scurvy. Friendly Indians gave them tea brewed from Vitamin C-rich branchlets of this cedar which cured their condition. Thus, the name tree of life was born.

Twigs are in attractive frond-shape sprays. Flat, scale-like leaves are in chain patterns, different from the round, sharp pointed, prickly needles of red cedar, *Juniperus virginiana*. Center leaf scales have a tiny button-like resin gland, the source of its characteristic fragrance. Branches grow vertically, not horizontally. Is this an adaptation to increase light exposure?

These trees range from Maine to Minnesota, south in the mountains to Tennessee, and in a few scattered bogs in northern Indiana, Illinois, and Ohio. They are essentially residents of cold boggy wetlands, swamps, and stream margins, and occasionally of limestone ridges. Not a native of Kalamazoo County, *Michigan Flora* records this cedar for Berrien and Cass counties in southwest Michigan. It is common above Muskegon and abundant in many square miles of the Upper Peninsula.

When trees are young, they grow in a narrow column and may develop multiple trunks during middle age. Like most evergreens, needles nearest the trunk mature and drop after four or five years leaving lower, older branches thin and bare. Trunks are often twisted and contorted.

Because white cedars prefer wet soil, their root structure is shallow. They are easy prey for high winds and frequently become wind-throws or tip-ups. Lying on wet soil, branches grow upright and take root creating impenetrable tangles of trunks, roots, and branches.

In Skegemog Swamp (a Michigan Department of Natural Resources and Nature Conservancy sanctuary east of Traverse City), you can use a boardwalk to study a typical cedar swamp. Only deer can navigate the dense and confused growth. White-tails get as much as twenty five percent of their food from these twigs and foliage. Their winter browse line is dramatic—a long line of trunks, all completely bare of foliage to a uniform height.

The thin bark, light yellowish gray, splits into frayed stringy strips. Older trunks develop narrow, muscular ridges and sturdy buttresses. A typical tree is thirty to sixty feet high. The national champion on South Manitou Island is almost five and a half feet in diameter and 113 feet tall—an aged giant.

Wind-pollinated flowers in May are so small as to be

almost invisible. Cones, too, are small, with only eight or ten scales, each with two winged seeds. Cheerful little pine siskins, cousins of American goldfinches, obtain much of their winter food from these tiny seeds.

A small- to medium-sized compact evergreen, white cedar's many varieties are widely used for ornamental purposes. The light, soft, and durable wood is used in boats and millwork. Decay resistant, it is suitable for fence posts, shingles, and railroad ties. Onondaga Indians called the tree Oosootah which means feather-leaf, and shredded the outer dry bark as tinder for fire by friction.

In a glacial relict Indiana bog, the state's only known site for this tree, the hundred or so white cedars appear to be root sprouts from older trees. There are no young ones.

November 20, 1990

Tulip Trees

The aristocratic tulip tree is among the many treasures of eastern woodlands. Its straight trunk, elegant flowers, truncated leaves, and cone-like fruits are not only unusual but also delightful.

Design and pattern in nature are always fascinating topics of conjecture. How does a trunk so straight and untapered come about? Why is its flower different from all other tree flowers?

Its scientific name, *Liriodendron tulipifera*, is so smooth it rolls right off one's tongue. *Liriodendron* means a tree bearing lilies and *tulipifera* means having tulips. Fossils from the Upper Cretaceous era, 70 to 100 million years ago, indicate that this tulip and a Chinese cousin are the only *Liriodendron*s to survive the Ice Age. European species were wiped out by glaciers.

These trees are found in rich moist soil east of the Mississippi River, except in New England and Florida. In Michigan, they grow most commonly south of the Grand River. In thickly wooded forests, straight trunks grow to great heights before branching. The handsome, symmetrical trees grow rapidly when young and mature at 200 years. This country's largest specimen grows in Virginia and is 363 inches in circumference and 124 feet tall.

Gray-brown bark of mature trees has corky ridges and is heavily furrowed. Four-lobed, smooth-edged leaves are broad like a maple's, but with the top seem cut off. On long stems, leaves wave in the wind like a poplar, hence the lumbermen's name of yellow poplar. But the tulip tree is not a poplar; it belongs to the magnolia family. In autumn, leaves turn a beautiful soft yellow and appear to be waxed.

A detail that never fails to attract me is the way leaves unfold. Terminal buds are flat, shaped like a duck's bill. When stipules (parts of the bill) separate, a curled-over leaf folded exactly on the midrib slowly straightens and unfolds, revealing a perfectly shaped miniature leaf. At its base inside the stipules is another duck's bill which also opens to disgorge another curled- over, folded-down-the-midrib leaf, and so on and on, ad infinitum.

After leaves are fully unfolded, singular flowers—tulips—open in late May or early June. Due to the tree's height and density of its foliage, they are hard to see. Dropped petals often are the first evidence of flowering. One summer, when I was studying at Kellogg Laboratories at Gull Lake, our botany professor was overjoyed when a high wind broke a large branch from a blossoming tulip tree. Students from around the country had plenty of material to make all the herbarium plates anyone could want. A rare opportunity.

Six petals of one and a half-inch flowers are yellow

with orange markings at their bases. Anthers are long and deep green. The flowers, laden with nectar, are favorites of the bees who make good honey from them. Hummingbirds also enjoy the nectar. Yellow-bellied sapsuckers drill rows of holes around trunks and obtain as much as two percent of their total food from the sap.

Cone-like seed structures are visible in the centers of flower cups from the outset. They grow and develop into aggregates of long, winged, overlapping blades with seeds enclosed at the base. This hard cone falls apart at maturity, often helped by hungry squirrels; large piles of seed remains accumulate around the tree base. In winter, cardinals and purple finches also eat tulip seeds.

The cone's central core and some outer parts remain upright until spring, resembling decorative candles on a large candelabra. A Pennsylvania mountainside, forested exclusively with tulip trees, is a beautiful sight when fresh snow crowns each and every one of tens of thousands of these candles.

Plant some tulip trees on your property as a unique gift of shade and ornamental beauty for your descendants.

May 21, 1989

Eastern Cottonwood

Have you looked at leaf buds on an eastern cotton-wood lately? You'll find they are reddish-brown, long, thin, pointed, shiny, and a little sticky. They grow at angles to stems, instead of close to twigs like most buds. Fragrant wax or resin seals and protects them from extreme cold and desiccation all winter, softening in spring when growth begins. This resin, also found on other poplars, was used medicinally for many years. Bees gather the softened wax, called propolis, and use it to seal cracks in their hives.

This tree, also called Carolina or necklace poplar, grows best in rich soils where roots stay wet, along prairie streams, and in sunny bottomlands. Under favorable conditions it may grow 80 to 100 feet tall with a massive trunk. Compared to oak trees which live 200 or 300 years, cottonwoods are not long-lived. They grow rapidly at first, and, according to John Eastman, as much as five feet in a year. The soft, weak wood and shallow root system, encouraged by a preferred high water table, make them frequent victims of high winds. Common associates are other flood plain and stream edge trees: black willow, sandbar willow, silver maple, red ash, American elm, northern hackberry, and box elder.

The American Forestry Association's champion in Wayne County, Michigan, is 148 feet tall and has a trunk twenty-six feet seven inches in circumference, measured four and a half feet from the ground.

Thick, glossy green leaves (three to six inches long) have curved teeth on the margins. The species name, *deltoides*, refers to both its triangular shape and the Greek letter Delta which is a triangle. Like its cousin the quaking aspen, cottonwood leaves have flexible flat stems as if they had been pinched. This allows blades to move freely in the wind. In autumn, waxy leaves turn brilliant yellow making great torches of the vase-shaped trees. Their bright gold is accented by scarlet Virginia-creepers often found enveloping large trunks.

Bark on saplings is smooth and greenish yellow, but develops unusual narrow sharp vertical ridges which later become confluent furrows.

Male flowers, appearing before leaves in March or early April, are borne in rusty catkins which grow longer and longer resembling tassels. They finally drop, liberally strewing sidewalks. Wind blows pollen to neighboring trees bearing all female flowers. Round green pea-sized beads of the less abundant, shorter, stiffer female catkins open later producing quantities of fluffy white down or cotton.

Tiny dark brown seeds attached to fine cotton threads, easily carried by the wind, are prolific. Eastman says: "Seeds readily germinate on bare, moist soil within a few hours of release, but few seedlings survive." Broken branches take root easily in moist soil.

The lightweight soft wood is used for boxes, household woodenware items, and paper pulp. In pioneer days on the prairie, treasured cottonwoods were often the only trees available. They provided logs for building homes and stockades, and shaded houses from a harsh sun. Their leaves were fed to stock. Cottonwoods are still planted in the west for wind and sun protection. Such windbreaks are essential to birds for shelter and nesting.

November 19, 1992

Hawthorns

Among wonders the rose family shares with us are hawthorns or thorn apple trees. They may be small, as trees go, but have many engaging, and not-so-engaging, characteristics.

One not-so-charming feature is the abundant, formidable, extremely sharp thorns. Deeply embedded in the pith of twigs, they do not break off easily as do raspberry or locust prickles, mere outgrowths of bark. Varying from species to species, they may be short or as much as four inches long, curved or straight, or even branched. General thorniness, heavy foliage, and thick branching make these trees preferred nest sites for many birds.

Charming traits are abundant showy flowers, attractive, shiny oval leaves, and bright colored fruit. Botanists estimate that there are from 100 to 1,200 native North American hawthorn species, with perhaps 1,500 worldwide. *Crataegus* is an extremely complex and difficult genus whose species have small variants in flower, leaf, or fruit that separate one cousin from another.

Hawthorns flower in May and June, simultaneously with leaves or later. Typical rose-shaped blossoms, petals are pink or white with 5, 10, 15, or even 25 stamens. Anthers may be white, yellow, pink, rose, or purple. The decorative fruit is red, yellow, blue, or even black. These little apples usually are round, but are sometimes pear-shaped with dry, mealy pulp containing from one to five seeds.

Fox sparrows and cedar waxwings are the chief seed eaters with northern bobwhites and ring-necked pheasants not far behind. Black bears and raccoons also enjoy hawthorn fruits. Uneaten ones may stay on the tree all winter. These trees are a good honey source, and nectar may even drop from blossoms. Bees probably cause extensive hybridizing.

Leaf shapes of each species are slightly different. Adding to the problem, a single tree may have leaves of different shapes. Edges are coarsely toothed. Variation prevails, challenging amateur and professional botanist alike. Deciduous leaves turn brilliant orange and red in fall, making them valuable in shrubbery borders.

Landscape architects are fond of hawthorns in small yards because of their distinct horizontal planes and their patterns of tortuous, somewhat zigzag branching. Most people are familiar with Washington hawthorn, a commonly planted ornamental tree. It has smooth, lobed, bright green leaves and large clusters of white blossoms followed by small, scarlet, edible haws. Native to southern states, it does well in the midwest and northeast. The *pauli* variety of the imported English hawthorn, or May tree, with bright scarlet, double flowers that grow in tiny gay corsages, is exceedingly attractive.

On stream banks, in pastures, and along roadsides, you find red haw or downy hawthorn. The first season's hairy twigs give it its name. Largest of all, it has a low conical crown. These trees are found in pastures where cattle and deer keep lower branches pruned by constantly browsing soft growth. Above grazing level, downies branch out to their usual wide-spreading shape creating bizarre, top-heavy trees. Stout, curved thorns may appear. The American Forestry Association says the largest hawthorn in the state is a downy at 8120 Macomb Street, Grosse Ile. The trunk's circumference, measured 4½ feet above ground level, is 105 inches; the height is 52 feet, and the crown spread is 62 feet.

The manual from which I learned my common trees 35 years ago devoted 44 of its 450 pages to hawthorn species, whereas the more important oaks had only 25. Modern books give a page or so to *Crataegus* species and refer you to technical treatises. For example, Charles Sargent's *Manual of the Trees of North America* devotes 36 pages of fine print and excellent drawings to details of 37 of the more easily separated species. Numbers of stamens and colors of anthers are the most helpful distinguishing characteristics.

The trees do well in most soils, even in clay, and thrive in sunny, exposed situations. The Kalamazoo Nature Center has a nice selection of varieties in its arboretum, including cokspur thorn, crimson cloud hawthorn, dotted hawthorn, single-seed howthorn, Toba hawthorn, Washington hawthorn, winter king hawthorn, downy hawthorn, American beauty hawhtorn, candied hawthorn, carmine hawthorn, Indian magic flowering hawthorn, profusion flowering hawthorn, Siberian haawthorn and snowcloud hawthorn.

I remember a rhyme in a charming old book of English nursery verses:

> The fair maid who the first of May
> Doth bathe her face in hawthorn dew
> Will ever after handsome be.

What did the Queen of the May do about the thorns?

May 22, 1990

Black Walnut

Michigan's champ is in Macomb County north of Detroit, but the state's southwest roads and fields are rich with many large specimens. The New Haven big one is 118 feet tall, with a crown spread of 116 feet and a circumference, 4 1/2 feet from the ground, of 232 inches.

The circumference of 7 large black walnut trees I measured in a friend's yard in Kalamazoo County read: 83, 83, 92, 104, 105, 110, and 126 inches. The 104-inch and 105-inch trees both had long, deep, lightning scars. In an old beech-maple forest is an edge-of-the-woods walnut giant with a circumference of 151 inches. One large low branch reaching to the light would itself be a large trunk in most settings. To think that this tremendous bulk all grew from one tough-shelled nut.

Leaves, shaped like feathers and arranged alternately, are long, 12 to 14 inches, with 15 to 23 stemless leaflets arranged oppositely. Leaflets are about 1 1/2 inches long and less than half as wide. They are thin and pointed with finely toothed edges, smooth above and lighter in color and slightly hairy below. The butternut tree, a close cousin, has longer leaves but fewer leaflets. Black walnut leaves, which have a hoof-shaped base, turn yellow in the fall and drop early, leaving branches decorated only with round green balls.

Bark of mature trees is dark and heavily furrowed by interesting, vertical ridges. Massive trunks support a few heavy horizontal branches from which numbers of green husked spheres begin to drop by early August.

Nuts are ripe and ready to eat in October, if you're strong and persistent enough to remove the husk and crack that thick, bony, deeply sculptured shell. We used to pour them out in our driveway to let the car's weight break husks. Their oil stains your hands for days and your clothes forever. Struggle for access is worthwhile because the meat is sweet and rich. Is there a tastier dessert anywhere than maple walnut ice cream?

Gray and fox squirrels gnaw walnuts into fragments to obtain meats. The feisty little red squirrel gnaws an irregular hole on either side of the shell. I think they earn their dinner the hard way.

Of the twelve species of *Juglans* in the world, six are native to this country. Our common black walnut extends through most of the east and into the prairies. In Michigan, it is common in the Lower Peninsula's southern half, rare in the northern half, and not found at all in the Upper Peninsula. Butternut is more common in the northeast. The remaining four species are found only in the west.

A pleasant open wide-spreading crown and general beauty impart significant ornamental value. Black walnut may not be a desirable lawn tree because its roots produce an allelopathic substance discouraging growth of some other plants. In simple terms, it sets up chemical warfare with tomatoes or rhododendrons. But along roadsides several large plants, notably burdock and pokeweed, grow close to those massive trunks.

These trees are comparatively free of plagues of leaf-eating insects. Their foliage is a favorite food for the ethereal pale green luna moth.

Because of long tap roots, trees may be difficult to transplant. However, we moved a fifteen-inch tall volunteer in mid-June that is doing well now. An easier way to have your own tree is to store nuts in gravel outside over winter, with a screen over the top to keep squirrels out. Jack Frost will crack that shell for you and have a seedling waiting, ready for its permanent home. Trees grow rapidly and are a valuable crop to plant if you have timber harvesting in mind. Black walnut wood is scarce, hardly available at any price. Friends have planted large acreages with black walnuts as an inheritance for their children. Will these be more reliable than a stock portfolio?

In *Trees Every Child Should Know*, Julia Rogers tells of early settlers clearing Ohio River bottomlands, cutting down and burning the great weed trees before plowing was possible:

> The stump of many a noble black walnut tree, cut down a century ago, has stood, undecayed, until recent years. So valuable is its wood that these stumps have been pulled up with expensive machinery, for the gnarly grained roots that are still sound.

Cut into thin sheets, the wood is used for veneering furniture.

America's favorite cabinet wood since colonial days, black walnut is still the wood of choice for gun stocks because it stands blows without splintering and takes a beautiful finish.

In case you're lucky, black walnut makes splendid long-lasting hot coals when used for campfire fuel.

August 8, 1991

Witch Hazel

To walk a southern Michigan woodland in late fall when witch hazel trees are in abundant flower is to walk a golden world. Since it is a small understory tree, you are surrounded by and right in among masses of purest yellow blossoms.

It grows best in sandy soil and can be found in oak-hickory or beech-maple woodlands, often in wet conditions or on moist slopes. The Haneses found *Hamamelis virginiana* near East, Goose, Pawpaw, and Sugarloaf lakes and in Cooper Township. Burton V. Barnes and Warren H. Wagner, in *Michigan Trees,* record its distribution as "common in the southern half of the lower peninsula; occasional in the northern one half of the lower peninsula; rare in the upper peninsula." Its wider range is a section of the country lying east of the 100th meridian, roughly in a line from eastern Texas to Minnesota's southeast. Slow-growing, shade tolerant, and short-lived, these trees are welcomed everywhere for their beauty.

Flowers grow in tousled clusters of three blossoms. Delicately fragrant, distinctive blossoms have narrow and waxy, bright yellow petals. Their unique, twisted ribbon shapes remind you of oriental brush paintings. Stamens form crosses in the bottoms of flower cups. Because flowers open as leaves fall, the entire tree soon appears yellow with petals unobscured. Everything else in the woods is going to sleep in the frosts and cold of October and November when witch hazel is in full blossom. We found lingering petals on a Christmas Day stroll.

While witch hazel is dropping yellowed leaves and spreading delicately fragrant flowers, it is also ripening last year's seed capsules. Stubby four-part pods have been developing since early spring. On reaching maturity, they split down the middle and forcibly eject two hard, shiny black seeds, a unique dispersal mechanism.

Thoreau wrote in his journal September 21, 1859:

> Heard in the night a snapping sound, and the fall of some small body on the floor from time to time. In the morning I found it was produced by the witch hazelnuts on my desk springing open and casting their seeds quite across my chamber, hard and stony as these nuts were. For several days they are shooting black seeds about my chamber.

If these little bullets happen to be launched as you walk past, you may think someone is shooting at you. On looking around, you'll find gaping seed pockets, yawning wide open. So forceful is ejection that seeds are thrown as far as twenty feet. Another one of Mother Nature's clever means of dispersal, this action assures that new trees are started at some distance from the parent. Empty capsules remain on trees all winter. Like pine cones, woody pods stay closed in rainy weather, but open to the sun. If you bring in a branch with the capsules showing slight openings, warm indoor air will speed maturing and you will experience a bombardment.

Dull, deep olive-green leaves, arranged alternately, are wavy margined and straight veined. Lopsided at the bottom, they grow two- to four-inches long. The hairless twigs are slender, often zigzag. The light gray brown bark is thin and smooth, becoming scaly with cross stripes. Inner bark has a purplish tinge.

In American folklore, a forked branch of witch hazel was a divining rod that told well witches where underground water supplies could be found. If you want to try your luck as a water witch, cut a small Y-shaped branch and grasp one tip in each hand, holding the main stem erect. Some say you should be blindfolded, but seeing or not, walk along the area where water is wanted. If the wand part bends down, this is the spot for your well.

Witch hazels, whether tree or shrub, one trunk or several, usually grow ten to twenty-five feet tall. The national champion is a Michigan specimen located near Muskegon. When measured in 1976, the trunk circumference was seventeen inches, height was forty-three feet, and the crown spread was forty-one feet.

Its wood, of no economic value, is hard, close-grained, and heavy. An Oneida Indian is credited with discovering that, by process of distillation, bark and twigs produce an extract useful as an astringent, muscle soother, or lotion. Indians made poultices from inner bark for inflamed eyes and itchy skin. Ernest Thompson Seton wrote that a snuff made from dried leaves would stop small cuts from bleeding.

Witch hazel has little wildlife value except to ruffed grouse and wild turkey who like its seeds, and to rabbits and squirrels who eat the bark, foliage, and seeds.

A southern cousin is vernal witch hazel which also has a topsy-turvy flowering schedule. Drive to the Nature Center parking lot in February amidst snow and ice. There you will find several large springtime shrubs in full blossom. Flowers are red-orange rather than golden yellow, and the petals perhaps not so pretty as fall-blossoming species, but any flower is much to be cherished in winter.

October 9, 1990

Birches

Now that leaves have fallen, it's fun to look around, study trees, and observe their distinctive characteristics. Most of us are familiar with the bark of white or paper birches which are abundant in upper Michigan, with a few occurring across the southern tier of counties.

Birches proved their usefulness in this country's early years. Logs were good heating fuel, the quality varying from species to species. Birch wood, which works easily, was fashioned into cups, bowls, snowshoe frames, and canoe paddles. A single large tree furnished material for a light waterproof canoe, some of which are still in use. Sheets of bark placed under shingles helped keep a log cabin snug, or covered a lean-to or tepee frame. Thin sections made excellent tinder or primitive writing paper.

European white birch is used in landscape plantings, but Barnes and Wagner wrote: "Unfortunately, this species is short-lived, apparently due to a combination of factors: it is not hardy in our climate, has a weak and shallow root system, and is subject to attack by stem borers."

Gray birch is a northeast native and occasionally appears out of range. Short-lived and extremely fertile, the twenty- to thirty-foot trees grow in groups of three and four trunks, all apparently coming from the same root. Its triangular leaves are longer and more narrowly pointed than paper birch. Obvious field marks, aside from large numbers of dangling fruiting cones, are black triangular patches on the trunk below each branch, patches not found on paper birch.

Gray birches grow on poor soils, often following fires. Like paper birch, the smooth bark is dark reddish brown the first few years, becoming white as the tree matures. Its bark peels in strips but not so easily as white birch does. My home is near a pure stand of gray birch where several hundred volunteers sprang up in an old cornfield not cultivated for twenty years. In winter, light cones, or strobiles, dance in the wind, dozens on a branch. Large flocks of American goldfinches move through, feeding on tiny seeds. The only problem we've noted is a severe insect infestation every June that turns all the leaves brown, but by mid-July new ones turn the woods green again.

In the palm of your hand, break apart a cone. In this inch-long cylinder you'll find many thin trefoil-shaped scales, or bracts, amid quantities of samaras, minute seeds set in wings of transparent tissue. Because the cone separates so readily, I often wonder how goldfinches trap the seeds before winds whisk them away. When the ground is snow covered, the number of beige scales and samaras visible on the surface is truly amazing. They pile up in miniature windrows along path edges. Preformed male catkins are already present on branches in August. In spring, these stretch out and provide pollen for the wind to carry to female flowers on the same tree.

An early childhood woodland favorite, white birch bark is one of the first nature items which children learn. Indian lore associated with it, plus year-round availability, increases its popularity over such favorites as acorns, pussy willows, and horse-chestnuts.

November 4, 1993

American Beech

Identifying trees by bark alone is difficult. The American beech, however, is one species with distinctive soft silvery blue-gray bark. It is so smooth and tight to the trunk that it invites carvings, a familiar vandalism. One observes that, truly, trees grow only at the top, because unsightly initials, hearts, and dates remain at eye level rather than disappearing upward and out of sight. And bears seeking flavorful nuts may leave permanent claw marks on trunks. On ancient trees, bark is usually rough and sectioned only around their elephant-feet basal roots.

In *A Countryman's Woods*, nature writer of unusual skill and sensitivity Hal G. Borland wrote:

> It was on a big beech in Washington County, Tennessee, that Daniel Boone carved his memorandum 'D. Boone cilled a bar on tree in year 1760.' That tree, incidentally, survived until 1916 and was estimated to be 365 years old, which gives an index to the longevity of the species.

Beeches are native to the entire eastern half of the country except Florida. In southwestern Michigan, growing with sugar maples, they identify a climax or steady state community. *Flora of Kalamazoo County* states that beech is "...a common tree in rich soil....Our beeches vary in leaf shape and in the color of the inner layers of wood." Fine stands grow along the Nature Center's Beechwoods and Marsh trails and in its Pioneer Farm woodland, south of DeLano Homestead. In its arboretum you can find two American beeches and several varieties of European beech.

Enormous trees that make you feel tiny are found in Berrien County's Warren Woods. Some are dying of great age, but their immense cylindrical trunks and tall, tall canopy never cease to amaze and delight visitors. The largest Michigan American beech is in Manistee: seventy-five feet tall, with a circumference, measured at four and a half feet from the ground, of one hundred seventy-two inches.

Buds are always easy to identify by their unique long and slim, sharp-pointed shape, like tiny cigars. Encased in shiny coppery gold membranes, they are visible at considerable distances in early spring woodlands that are still brown, still asleep. Lateral buds stick straight out from twigs in an unusual fashion. As their scales fall away, lovely fan-pleated leaves hang limp.

Paper-thin oval leaves are from four to six inches long and from one to two and a half inches wide. Edges have incurved teeth at the end of each vein. Both surfaces are smooth; upsides are a rich, dull bluish-green, and undersides lighter and shiny. Borland wrote that leaves are almost translucent, letting light through but not heat.

In autumn, the leaves turn a warm coppery brown and then a glorious yellow, catching and holding light. Many, like others of the Fagaceae family, cling until spring growth forces them to drop in April. This is especially noticeable on young trees or on outer branches of older ones. During winter, these leaves bleach to a warm ivory and become tissue thin. Graceful little saplings with their gauzy winter attire always remind me of ballerinas dancing through woodlands.

Since good nut production occurs only every three to five years, beeches do not sheet forest floors with a large number of young trees in the manner of their constant companions, sugar maples. Triangular nuts occur in pairs in attractive soft spiny burs. Birds and mammals enjoy the sweet nuts, as did extinct passenger pigeons and pioneers' hogs in the eighteenth and nineteenth centuries. Barnes and Wagner wrote that the nuts often do not contain a fertile seed, further explaining American beech's low reproductive rate.

These trees are shade tolerant and grow best in acid soils with ample surface moisture to support shallow root systems. Suckers on extensive roots are frequent and the common means of reproduction. At Robinson's Woods in Berrien County we were intrigued by a relict hollow stump about three feet high. The trunk's center had rotted completely leaving only a three-inch thick bark ridge from which a dozen twenty-foot saplings emerged.

An old tree book from 1909 claims that beeches never are struck by lightning. Can this be so?

June 20, 1991

149

Mighty Bats from Little Ashes Grow

One of the tallest, straightest trunks in forests is that of the stately white ash. Its bark is dark gray-brown; that of older trees is characterized by deep furrows whose narrow channels are diamond shaped. Learn to recognize these diamonds. No other tree has such regularly intersecting flat ridges; they are a foolproof field mark. Bark from older trees tends to become corky.

Branching of city grown trees begins low on trunks. Crowns are oval, making them pleasing shade trees for lawns. Root systems are wide-spreading and often deep. When you find these ashes in woodland areas, branching is restricted to the upper parts of trunks where sunlight penetrates.

Leaves are opposite, feather-compound, and divided into 5 to 7 short stalked small leaflets which do not leave a scar when removed from the midrib. The leaf itself leaves a large and distinctive deeply notched, half-round scar on the twig. They are 8 to 12 inches long, with oval leaflets measuring 3 to 5 inches. Undersides are whitish, paler than the shiny upsides. This is the source of the name. Edges are generally smooth, untoothed. Thick, firm leaflets turn shades of yellow and plum in autumn when photosynthesis stops.

Ash branches are also opposite, an occurrence in only a few tree families. If leaves and branches are arranged alternately, the tree is not in these families. Such characteristics are particularly useful in winter when other clues are scarce. A handy phrase to help you remember opposite arrangements in woody plants is MAD-Cap-Horse: *M*aple *A*sh *D*ogwood-*Cap*rifoliaceae-*Horse* chestnut. (Caprifoliaceae: the honeysuckle family)

Flowers, opening in May before leaves unfold, are small and rather uninteresting, borne in loose, conspicuous clusters. Like most wind-pollinated ones, there are no petals, only a minute, green, tubular calyx. Male flowers have two or three stamens; females have one two-celled ovary. The sexes grow on separate trees.

Samaras are uniquely shaped, resembling canoe paddles. The handle bears a plump, round seed and the winged blade is designed to help wind and water distribute it. White ash seeds occupy about one third of the samara's one and a half inches; those from red and green ash trees use half the paddle length. Fruits, often having a reddish cast, hang in crowded clusters and frequently cling through winter.

Cardinals, evening grosbeaks, and cedar waxwings may get as much as two percent of their food from these seeds. Rodents and wild turkeys shuck the blade and eat only the seed. Because the clusters remain through the winter, they are useful late in the season when ground level foods have been consumed or are buried under snow.

White ash is found from Nova Scotia to southern Minnesota, south to Texas and Florida. It is common in the Lower Peninsula and decreases in numbers as one goes north and west in Michigan. The Haneses listed it as "a common tree in all county forests."

Oak and hickory trees are frequent companions in the upland sites white ash prefers; it does not like poorly drained sites and flood plains where its cousin, the black ash, flourishes. It is less frequent in beech-maple woodlands.

The largest white ash in Michigan, located in Lenawee County, southwest of Detroit, also happens to be the national champion specimen. When measured recently, it stood 114 feet tall with a circumference, at 4½ feet, of 20 feet 5 inches. Something about its growing condition really pleased this tree because white ash usually grows 50 to 80 feet tall and 3 feet around. Under favorable conditions, these trees grow rapidly and may be 45 feet tall by their 30th birthday.

Barnes and Wagner wrote:

> Moderately shade-tolerant; moderately fast-growing; moderately long-lived. Leaves flush late in the spring and are among the first to drop in autumn. Sprouts readily following injury by fire, cutting, or browsing... Relatively free of major insect and disease pests.

Of the sixteen ash species native to North America, the hard, strong wood of white ash makes it the most important commercially. Campers like it because it produces hot coals, ideal for broiling. An early writer noted that inner bark was useful for writing paper. And Francois André Michaux, a Frenchman who botanized in North America from 1785 to 1797, wrote that a leaf rubbed on a bee sting or mosquito bite relieves itching at once. Worth trying, isn't it?

Due to its elasticity and tough close grain, tool handles, skis, and tennis rackets are made from this wood. The more it is rubbed, the smoother it becomes. The wood is brown with lighter colored sapwood and is used for furniture, oars, and interior finish of buildings. Second only to oak in worth, it is a valuable American lumber tree.

But most of us think of white ash as the source for that great American traditional staple, the baseball bat. Where would sluggers be without their favorite?

September 11, 1990

Of Scenes
and Seasons

Marvels of Design and Pattern

As you roam the natural world, are you aware of the entrancing patterns and designs in leaves and flowers, sea shells and ice crystals, and windblown sand ripples? What of the majesty of cream puff cumulus clouds piled mass on mass, drifting lazily in a blue, blue sky?

What is lovelier than feathery fringes on an unfurling gentian petal? Or minute flutings on the leading edge of an owl's wing which allow it to fly so silently? Is there anything more amazing than the singular beauty of a snowflake and the incredible fact that no two are ever alike? How can there be such mind-boggling infinitesimal diversity? Or, conversely, how can a ginkgo tree in October shed 10,000 or 100,000 golden fans all shaped exactly the same?

How can some crinoids, the 500 million-year-old sea lily fossils we find on Lake Michigan beaches, have perfect five-pointed stars in their middle? Have you enjoyed the star in an apple halved at its equator? Who can forget Georgia O'Keeffe's magnificent *White Trumpet Flower* with a star glowing deep in its heart? Look at the spreading star of the marsh-marigold seed.

Is there a bell shape more pleasing than that of diminutive pink twinflowers, a favorite of Linnaeus and premier performer of the Canadian carpet? Relish the elegant architectural grace of water-plantain, even of sterile common horsetail stalks.

How can ferns unwind their fiddleheads so exquisitely in early spring? How do tiny rootlets, spun endlessly by dune winds, inscribe splendid arcs, even perfect circles, in sand? How do wild cucumber vine tendrils become tightly wound spiral tubes?

Large globular goat's beard seeds exceed the dandelion's in perfect symmetry of spun gold filaments. Aren't dew drops on orb spider webs one of the most wondrous things under our skies? The web itself is a design and engineering marvel, and dew enhances each strand.

How can mushrooms and fungi emerge in such a dazzling array of forms and textures? Their colors range from inky black to brilliant oranges and yellows of sulfur polypores. Even deadly *Amanita* is a perfect colorful orb as it emerges. Tiny scarlet cup is an early harbinger of spring in a hardwood forest. Unique earth stars flourish in sterile, sandy soils. A single spherical puffball fills a bushel basket. Toadstool shapes are familiar to all, but watch for trumpets of chanterelles, strange phallic forms of stinkhorns, delicately fluted fans of woody turkey tails, and fragile corals in white, pink, orange, and red. Endless designs.

Carefully carve away sand around a burrowing spider's hole to find a neatly spun tubular web twelve to fifteen inches long, his clever way of escaping surface heat. Or enjoy concentric convolutions of freezing patterns in shallow puddles and streamlets, the beauty of repetitive line. Hoarfrost on window panes exceeds tropical forests in lushness of frond shapes.

Why do bees and wasps fashion precise hexagonal shapes? Why not round or irregular? Why does the rare seaside-spurge often grow in a perfect circle? Why does Baltic rush grow in straight lines?

Grasses give us some of our most beautiful designs and patterns, often in microcosm. Marram and Junegrass seed stalks trap morning dew to let the sun practice dancing. A tawny field of little bluestem's furry stars is an autumn delight. How does beach-three awn grass know to form spirals at a specific stage of maturation? Alpine or arctic fields of cotton grass in full blossom, nodding in a persistent breeze, are memories to cherish.

One September morn, I found 210 black-bellied plovers resting in a Cape Cod salt marsh, every bird standing on one leg, and everyone faced into the wind at the same angle. Unforgettable.

Seed pods from all members of the milkweed family demand our admiration. Dissect a green pod to see the orderly arrangement of seed and parachute. Count them. Could you package 100 or 200 or more seeds and their filmy delights in one little pod? Could you design it so all fluffy filaments are imprisoned until the last minute, until the pod dries and splits to the tip, guaranteeing those diaphanous masses waving from bare stalks?

A luminous crescent moon low in a sunset afterglow

is perhaps nature's most graceful manifestation of a curvilinear shape.

Occasionally you will find a leaf whose green substance was eaten by an insect or eroded by time, leaving only a life-giving network of veins, a fascinating, intricate pattern. There must be miles of such unseen reticulation in leaves of a single tree.

Soft antennae of moths are as delicate as the infinitely fine feathers which make up a bird's eye ring.

A walk along a sandy beach reveals ever-changing wave imprint designs. Tiny bits of sand and matter deposited by each receding wavelet create graceful undulating lines, lines suggestive of a contemplative Chinese brush painter.

There are some things you can never see from the ground. As I took off from the Winnipeg airport one evening, the setting sun illumined not one, not two, but three huge and perfect oxbows in an old river bed below me, a glistening undulant line.

The sum of these observations is nature's glory. Turn on your sensitivity. See what new patterns you can ferret out for your own pleasure. As Philip Hyde once wrote, "Let the land get close to you."

November 13, 1988

Clouds

One of the strange and memorable delights of long distance airplane flights is going up and up through endless marshmallow fluff and then suddenly coming out into a spectacular burst of light. In all directions, as far as one can see, stretches a flat white surface, sheets and sheets of cloud tops.

Pilots have intensive training in the complicated ways of clouds; they are important as significant indicators of flying conditions. They give evidence of moisture content and of the stability of the atmosphere. A cloud of water droplets may be friendly, but one of freezing ice crystals must be treated with respect.

Those of us who stay on the ground can also profit from sky watching, both practically and aesthetically. Those who live in the midwest belt experience the lowest number of hours of sunshine in the whole country. Clouds are always with them--high, low, and in between. Proximity to Lake Michigan affects southwest Michigan weather. Clouds moving over the lake are warmed by the water and absorb more moisture. Over cooler land, they drop it, giving the all too familiar lake effect storms particularly noticeable in the snow season.

Meteorologists classify clouds according to their appearance and height above the earth, and these dozen types often merge into each other. Most of us have trouble with specific identifications, but we know enough to observe safety precautions when black clouds are approaching packing wind, snow, or thunderstorms. A whirling black funnel cloud doesn't need a name to make us seek shelter rapidly.

I can tell when I'm inside a cloud and am able to define that as fog. One of my favorite occupations in the mountains is watching fog creep up the valleys as evening falls and slither out again in morning sun. I like to walk in fields on early summer mornings when patchy pillows of fog sit a foot or two above the green. What holds them up? What makes the mass creep? Carl Sandburg once wrote: "Fog comes on little cat feet."

I can tell if a stratus cloud is so low that it is raining and, therefore, it is called nimbus. I have difficulty deciding whether an amorphous white mass way above me is at 6,500 feet or 20,000 feet or somewhere in between. Sometimes I can tell when vague trailing clouds are really diffusing airplane vapor trails.

So-called high clouds have their bases at 20,000 feet, rise to 40,000, and are made of ice crystals. Cirrus clouds are delicate wisps or plumes seen against a blue sky. They may be feathers or streaks with upturned ends, called mares' tails. These usually mean a pleasant day is at hand. Another familiar high cloud, cirrocumulus, consists of rounded masses or flakes with no shadows and is often arranged in ripples. Sometimes these look like fish skeletons. When the sky has a ground glass appearance with the sun or moon visible through a milky veil, thin altostratus clouds prevail. They may be steely gray covering the heavens and may shift into nimbostratus storm clouds.

Low clouds occur from earth's surface to above 6,500 feet and may contain either water or ice forms. Stratus clouds, as the name implies, are in uniform layers with no markings. Their base is often ragged, making height hard to determine. Scattered stratus clouds are the delight of sunset photographers.

The form most of us prefer above all others, the dense fair-weather cumulus cloud, has vertical development starting at 1,500 feet and rising higher. These are the big cream puffs, the castles we see floating through a cerulean canopy on an idyllic summer day. Their billowy, sparkling white cushions are usually grayed toward their flat horizontal bottoms. Cauliflower-like shadows and valleys define little puffs, new cells, nestled in the fluff. Curving edges and contours of heaped clouds are well defined. Dorothy Aldis wrote of such summer delights:

> If I had a spoon
> As tall as the sky
> I'd dip out the clouds
> That go sailing by.
> I'd take them right in
> And give them to cook
> And see if they tasted
> As good as they look.

Cumulus clouds form characteristically during daytime and dissipate by night. They drift slowly, like floats in a big parade, or sometimes are stationary for long periods. I especially like watching when a lower more amorphous set of grayer clouds moves by faster than the bright light-filled, firmly edged cumulus puffs lying behind them, all against a blue sky. The ever-shifting contrasts in texture are the charm of this hide-and-seek game.

O'Keeffe, with her usual sophisticated simplification, painted superb pictures of the sky as seen from an airplane. Her twenty-four foot painting, *Sky Above Clouds IV*, hangs in The Art Institute of Chicago.

Try your hand at classifying cloud forms; it's harder than you think. Since we can't do anything about the weather, we might as well enjoy observing and understanding its signposts.

October 14, 1995

Rain

Rain is much in the public eye these days as forest losses from acid rain and widespread destruction of rain forests are matters of serious concern. News of both are featured in the media while scientists, officials, and conservationists the world over struggle for answers.

Acid rain is a term coined 120 years ago when a British chemist observed a prevalence of sooty air in Manchester. Soon, others learned that forests and rivers were affected negatively by sulfur dioxide emissions from coal burning. Statues and public buildings which had stood for many years suddenly showed signs of their stones corroding.

Widespread areas of the Black Forest's coniferous trees in southwest Germany, perhaps seventy percent, have suffered serious deterioration. The evidence is reduced resistance to insect pests and fungi, resulting in yellowed or absent needles and early death.

Motor vehicle emissions add to residues from coal, oil, and natural gas burning, and increase sulfur and nitrogen oxides in the air. These pollutants react with moisture to produce sulfuric and nitric acids. Droplets are transported by rain, mist, snow, or even dust, wherever prevailing winds blow them. The United States and Canada, particularly the northeastern sections, are suffering with heavy forest loss. There are other damaging side effects beside forest death: smog and acidified lakes. Polluted waters poison entire ecosystems, killing insects, salamanders, mussels, perch, bass and trout in thousands of lakes, also affecting fish-eating birds such as terns and ospreys. Research is in progress to determine the cause of frequent bill deformities among Lake Michigan's cormorants. In affected areas, frogs, toads, and salamanders are dying or producing deformed embryos.

Anna Comstock in her *Handbook of Nature Study*, published in 1911, wrote extensively about rain and snow but nowhere mentioned acid rain, further evidence of late twentieth century damage to the earth.

Both tropical and temperate zones have rain forests, areas in which heavy rains and coastal fogs produce phenomenally dense or tall tree populations supporting an incredible variety of plants. I've not experienced a tropical rain forest but memories of the temperate ones of Washington's Olympic Peninsula and of British Columbia's Pacific Coast, both aided by 80 to 180 inches of rain annually, are "Color me Green." Where 300-foot Sitka spruces, Douglas firs, shrubs, vines, and sword ferns didn't cover every inch, lush mosses filled cracks and crannies, creating eerie, yellow-green filtered-light woodlands where the only sound was rushing water. Banana size slugs relished the dampness. The Olympic rain forest has the greatest weight of vegetation per acre in the world. Tropical forests have a greater diversity of species, but not the immense trees.

It is unfair for us to criticize Third World countries as they seek food and jobs by burning or lumbering, because we completely logged our original forests in New England and Michigan. The Amazon rain forest is particularly rich in unidentified species of possible medicinal or nutritional use, but is already ten percent destroyed. Scientists warn us that the world's rain forests have been reduced to half their original extent. We must ensure that the remaining ones are treated responsibly as a renewable resource.

Kalamazoo County averages thirty-five inches of rain a year, providing decent living conditions for humans and ample moisture for good growth of trees and crops. It's hard for me to imagine what life would be like with eighty inches of rain pelting down or, conversely, ten inches or less on deserts and arctic tundra.

There is no new water on earth. What we have was here a century or a thousand centuries ago, reconstituted and redistributed. We must husband it for its best uses.

October 29, 1994

Pré

Can you imagine how seventeenth century French explorers reacted when they first saw our vast and track-less prairies? Overawed, they would have compared them with their country's smaller open spaces and named them pré, their word for meadow.

When someone says prairie to you, what images come to mind? A dull expanse of landscape? Grazing herds of bison? Fields of grasses? Indians hunting? Leaping flames of raging fires?

How do you know a prairie when you see one? To the unknowing, it's that old weed patch. But catch a glimpse of big bluestem or a spike of white false indigo and you've found a true indicator. Varying soil and rainfall support different typical grassland species. Prairies are classified by topography, amount of moisture, or soil composition. Here is one scientific definition: prairie has less than one mature tree per acre, and at least half the vegetation is grasses. It is also home to such characteristic flower families as aster and pea.

Early season plants are small: pussytoes, pasque-flower, prairie smoke, and bird-foot violet. In summer, a virgin prairie may have seventeen kinds of flowers blossoming each week with 300 possible in such large expanses as The Nature Conservancy prairies in Kansas and South Dakota. By autumn, when waving grasses are six to ten feet tall, compass-plants and prairie dock wave conspicuous yellow flowers aloft.

Prairie plants have developed such qualities as stiff, nonwilt stems, sticky sap that resists evaporation, and hairy leaves or stems that retain moisture and reflect sunlight. The leaves are long and narrow and often are held upright, preventing overheating. They may be deeply lobed, often prickly or covered with a waxy substance, or thick with in-rolled edges preserving moisture.

Nearly two-thirds of a plant grows below ground, a unique feature which allows most prairie communities to survive despite frequent fire, periods of drought, extremes of temperature, and steady animal grazing. Crowns are heavy and thick and marvelously interlocking roots as long as five to ten feet are common. Some grasses, particularly cord grass of swamp edges, spread roots over the surface of the soil creating solid mats.

Where can you go to see a prairie plot? The March-April 1988 issue of *Michigan Natural Resources Magazine* has a fine article by Tom Huggler, containing delightful pictures and locations of Michigan prairies. The state's southwest section has remnant bits and pieces of land where original grassland plants still grow in what is known as the prairie peninsula. A few scraps of old prairie are scattered as far east as Saginaw. Throughout the state, several areas have been restored or reconstructed.

Our richest prairie lands have been farmed intensively for more than a century. Sturdy plants have hung on tenaciously in pioneer cemeteries, along railroad rights of way, and in scattered tracts that escaped plowing. Such early Michigan beauties as blue-hearts and soapwort gentian are gone forever and prairie orchids are in serious trouble. Even the stunning Michigan lily is becoming hard to find.

Prairies have their own niches for insect, bird, and mammal communities. Many species are in danger as remaining units become smaller and smaller. Prairie chickens are lost to us because of the destruction of their booming ground habitat where their mating dances took place. Some 60 million bison were killed by immigrants, a result of greed for hides, meat, and land.

Learning interesting components of prairie life, preserving bits of original prairie in old cemeteries and along railroad tracks, and establishing restorations and reconstructions help us maintain flora and fauna diversity. It keeps our traditions alive and aids understanding of and respect for our pioneer ancestors and heritage.

May 29, 1988

Prairie Grass Heritage

In *Michigan Flora*, Voss devotes 133 pages to grasses including both native and introduced species. The kinds are too many and distinctions in tiny flowers are often too technical for most of us, but let's look at a few of the more distinctive.

Seeds of many grasses were planted at the Kalamazoo Nature Center's prairie reconstruction in 1976. Most have thrived and are beautiful now. You can walk unseen among gently moving big turkey foot stalks waving six-to nine-feet-tall. Fuzzy three-branched seed heads, a soft bronzy red, give this plant one of its common names. The stem's lower part remains blue-green, a source of its other common name, big bluestem. Voss maps this species in forty-six of the sixty-five lower peninsula counties, noting that it is found in oak woods, jack pine plains, old fields, and bog borders, as well as in prairie remnants.

Silhouetted against intense blue cloudless autumn skies, these tall grasses are a reminder of their importance in our national history and daily lives. They dominated the tall grass prairie and were more common in lowland areas than in drier uplands. Great lumbering bison, or buffalo, herds thrived on big bluestem's nutritious stems. Growing for 10,000 years, its six-foot-deep roots became tangled into dense masses.

A serious problem in the 1800-1840 settlement period was breaking up the centuries-old sod. Pioneer farmers struggled to pull wooden moldboard plows through big turkey foot. Early drawings show a clumsy plow with two small cartwheels drawn by five pairs of oxen. Few could afford to hire the oxen and the required three-man team. Instead, the farmers broke up small amounts themselves, a little more each year until John Deere invented a self-cleaning steel plow in 1837. By 1843, Deere was annually selling a thousand of his unique implements. This spelled the end of vast open vistas. Our prairie heritage became a lost landscape, replaced by today's monoculture scene of agribusiness corn factories.

Early settlers lacked wood to build homes, barns, and fences. Cottonwood and willow dominated watercourses, a far cry from the oak, hickory, and walnut they had known back east. Prairie sod was an acceptable, if unattractive, substitute; dense roots of slough grass were cut into slabs a foot wide and two feet long for human and livestock shelters. Walls were weatherproof, cool in summer and warm in winter, made so by placing pieces two sods wide and alternating layers at right angles. Thatched roofs were less successful. Heavy rain and melting snow kept the dirt floors damp. Water, as well as timber, was often scarce but the fertility of the land made sacrifices worthwhile.

By the 1870s, when transportation improved and

building materials became available, soddies vanished. The 1989 North Dakota centennial postage stamp shows a sod house.

Today, corn and soy bean fields delineate and replace the big bluestem prairies. Only one tenth of one percent of the original remains. In Prairie Ronde Cemetery, south of Kalamazoo, big bluestem still clusters among gravestones from the 1830s and 1840s.

Native grasses add much to our autumn scene. A midgrass, little bluestem with charming fluffy florets, survives in much drier habitats than its taller cousin. It grows in sandy or rocky soil, sending its roots down only three or four feet. It actually is blue stemmed only in early summer. By the time delicate, fuzzy seeds emerge in September, stalks of mature plants are reddish brown, wine red, and orange. These rich colors remain well into winter when they fade to reddish tan. Excellent forage plants, these two species made up three-quarters of midwest prairie cover. Growing from the base of the stem, they are not damaged by grazing.

Canada wild rye has a densely flowered, rather bushy seed head which nods gracefully in the wind making it easy to recognize. It grows in tufts in dry or moist soil and survives overgrazing and trampling better than any other prairie species.

Indian grass, equally showy and as tall as big turkey foot, develops a shiny golden plume when pollinating. Later, stems and seeds turn a warm bronze. Small twisted bristles grow on each flower.

In *Where the Sky Began*, John Madson wrote about

midwestern prairies:

> A big patch of tall *Sorghastrum* is the ultimate play-
> ground. The kids are safely lost in deep grass that
> soaks up their noise and energy, finally spewing
> them out tired, quieter, and almost human. Another
> plus for prairie.

September 17, 1989

Bogs

Southern Michigan has a goodly number of bogs, glaciated depressions with restricted drainage and cold saturated soils. Extensive carpets of sphagnum moss plants maintain highly acidic conditions with a pH of less than five. Organic soils are mainly peat with underlying masses of dead sedges and are low in nutrients, especially available nitrogen. Small open water areas are common and often contain interesting insectivorous bladderwort species.

Quaking bogs are found in glacial relict kettle lakes and develop when submerged plants, over a period of time, form unstable networks of roots and plant parts. These may start as floating islands or just as extensions of shore lines. Low shrubs, evergreen trees, tamarack, bog birch, and red maple, slowly become established as the half-live, half-dead mat thickens and consolidates. Poison sumac is characteristic. Beware.

Thick sphagnum moss mats are saturated, often floating and unstable. You can walk on their flexible surfaces, which undulate like a waterbed, but breakthroughs are possible. Sphagnum is an unusual genus with hundreds of different species, of which six or eight may be found in southwest Michigan. They may be green, red, or yellow-green. All have amazing liquid retaining capacity, able to tenaciously hold fifteen to twenty times their weight in water. Just squeeze a fragment to see the water flow.

Because bog waters are so acidic and low in minerals, plant species are limited in number. Many are northern species, probably remnants of postglacial vegetation, already adapted to simple living.

Leatherleaf, an early flowering shrub, is tolerant of high acid, low mineral conditions. It may cover vast areas like Bishop Bog in Portage. Heath family members (bog-rosemary, azalea, and swamp laurel) do especially well. Blueberries and cranberries thrive at the city's West Lake Nature Preserve.

A half-dozen sedge species, growing in hummocks, are characteristic, particularly the graceful and conspicuous cotton-grasses.

Such orchids as rose pogonia, grass-pink, yellow fringed orchid, and moccasin-flower often do well; they have suffered serious overpicking despite Michigan's do not pick law. We found a few tiny dragon's mouth orchids in West Lake Bog in May 1991.

Chain ferns like bogs, too. Royal and marsh ferns often thrive around the edges. But the most interesting species are insectivorous plants whose unique adaptations enable them to survive severe conditions. Pitcherplant is the most dramatic of these with its long-stemmed, nodding red blossoms and leaves modified into vases, or pitchers, which attract, trap, and drown insects. The enzyme-laden liquid in the pitcher absorbs and digests needed minerals from its tiny prey.

Minute rosettes of sundew have gluey gland-tipped hairs which attract, wrap, and thus trap insects. Recent experiments with radioactive isotopes prove that minerals from flies wind up in sundew roots. Botanists have worked at solving the mysteries of these spectacular plants for more than 300 years. Experiments have been many and various, and many conclusions were far from today's truths.

You won't find snails, worms, or crayfish in bogs. You will see birds and mammals similar to those in other wetlands, but they are usually fewer in number. The restricted plant life reduces food choices.

June 24, 1993

A Day In June

What is so rare as a day in June, especially when someone else is paddling you down the placid Kalamazoo River shortly after dawn?

A pale crescent moon looks down on one peaceful wild vista after another. This scene must not always be serene because water stains on tree trunks are two feet above today's river level.

In Allegan County the river is wide and placid. Even though it's running fairly high, the current is visible only where unseen snags cause it to ripple, to swirl and boil up.

One bright clump of yellow iris stands out against the verdant dense shore vegetation. A European garden escapee, this vivid flower is becoming much at home on midwest river banks.

Barn swallows nesting under the highway bridge swoop through floating mist, puffs made luminescent by pale dawn light. Metal pole barns have deprived these swallows of their traditional nesting places, but they seem to be adapting.

A great blue heron floats along leisurely, emerging

now and then from ghostly mists. His bowed wings, with a magnificent seven-foot spread, move with steady rhythmic grace as if timed by a metronome. A belted kingfisher rattles stridently, on the prowl for his fishy breakfast, as he moves down the river from one lookout point to another.

Mile after mile there is no sign of man or his handiwork; all is silence, save for bird song. A cardinal whistles frequently and a scarlet tanager sings his sore-throated robin notes. A yellow-throated vireo, hidden in treetop foliage, chants lustily, ending with his husky signature *three eight* note. Green headed mallards lounge in shallows and song sparrows, the river's most common bird, call frequently.

Occasionally a large, bare sand bank edges the river but most shores are thickly forested with willows, silver maples, black walnuts, and flowering black cherries. In one sandy bluff, bank swallows dart in and out of their holes, chattering noisily. What a perilous existence to raise one's young in sand burrows.

Common yellowthroat's *witchity witchity* rings out more and more frequently as the sun rises higher and mists creep away.

Peeling, cream colored bark of sycamores shows up plainly amid otherwise dense green. Several are large with thick, heavily foliaged branches. Some trunks lie flat, parallel with the river or out in it, undermined but still living. Ruby-throated hummingbirds like to nest in these sleeping giants.

River-bank grape and poison ivy, our northern

equivalents of Spanish moss, festoon the occasional basswood and oak. Heavy vines not only provide tasty seasonal foods, but also prime nesting spots. A white pine here and there adds different texture and color interest to the scene.

Where old mossy windfall logs reach out into the river, soil and vegetable matter pile up. In these catchalls, colonies of handsome native lizard's tail and aggressive alien garlic mustard become established. The latter is more often a woodland invader, but here it luxuriates in quiet corners down the full length of the river.

Other visible flowers are a few bright patches of Canada anemone, occasional multiflora rose, and highbush cranberry shrubs.

Northern orioles are brilliant flashes against the green. Their lovely high whistle is delightful. A caroling of a wood thrush echoes across the water. The loveliest bird call of all? Very likely. The indigo bunting clinks out his spinning silver dollar song in metallic pairs.

Winding, gently winding, here a curve, there a curve, on and on the quiet river flows. Miles and miles of lush loveliness. A bullfrog *chugarums* from a cattail area in a dusky backwater cove.

June 30, 1994

Ottawa Marsh

Ottawa Marsh, in Allegan County, is an immense flood plain area created many years ago by flooding a woodland with Kalamazoo River water. A canoe trip in late spring is a wonderful nature adventure.

The marsh is a veritable moonscape, populated only with silent sentinels, tall, tall, trunks of dead trees now bleached white from years of full exposure to the sun. All branches are long gone. It is Michigan's own great Dismal Swamp. No living trees remain, only acres of scattered islets of thousands of bullheads and fragrant water lilies. What a strange landscape. I wonder what it's like in winter.

The water level is too low to float a canoe after July fourth. Even in June it grounds occasionally. One strong agile paddler in rubber boots is a necessity.

Thrashing carp or suckers make the only sound except for bird song and a faraway drilling of a pileated woodpecker. The sound or sight of this crow-sized bird with the flaming scarlet crest never fails to increase a birder's heart rate.

Oddly, for all the exposed dead logs, no turtles were

seen. Too early in the day? Too cool? Painted and map turtles do live here.

Birds are everywhere, especially tree swallows, swooping and darting, mating in air. We saw yellow-billed cuckoos, warbling vireos, scarlet tanagers, American robins, blue jays, yellow warblers, eastern kingbirds, cedar waxwings, and nine wood ducks. On another trip, the stern paddler saw an eastern bluebird pair nesting, quite a change from their usual open field habitat.

I wonder at the absence of duckweed. It is so common in most quiet southwest Michigan waters. The absence of black terns is puzzling, too. Their numbers are dwindling as a result of loss of wetlands. This serene isolated area, with islands of low cover, seems ideal nesting and feeding habitat. My informant says black terns are usually here, that nests may have been washed out in early high water.

Red-winged blackbirds and tree swallows dart among rafts of lavender pickerel-weed flower stalks. The stern paddler, an experienced bird counter with acute hearing, estimated 155 redwings and 110 tree swallows. Redwings are the largest group of summer avian residents; tree swallows are second and common grackles third. Our day's trip census totaled fifty-five species.*

In the distance, in tops of tall dead trees, we saw the great blue heron's extensive nesting colony. My paddler,

* *The bird censusing conducted in Ottawa Marsh is part of the total research project studying breeding birds of the Kalamazoo River, undertaken by the Kalamazoo Nature Center research staff.*

who stood in the canoe and held binoculars steady, counted eighty-one nests and estimated a total of 125 to 150. Long necks of the young rose above large stick nests. The parents were away feeding, or perched nearby, out of reach of the clamor. I always marvel at the habits of this tall bird with long, gangly legs. He conducts all family affairs, courtship, mating, nest-building, egg-laying, sheltering and feeding of young, high in tree tops, while tiny warblers nest in security and comfort on or near the ground.

At last, a prothonotary warbler! For forty years of birding I've longed for a really good look at this intensely golden songster. Here he is, sitting outside his nest hole in a bare stump and singing *zweet zweet zweet* all on one note. This flooded wooded bottom land is his favorite habitat.

When we pulled into the landing area at Wing Little Point, visible plant populations changed suddenly. Instead of native plant species dominating the marsh, we found many aliens. Burdock, garlic mustard, multiflora rose, and deadly nightshade thrived, unpleasant evidence of human intrusion. Weedier sand country natives were there too: poison ivy, ragweed, *Impatiens*, bracken fern, stinging nettle, gray dogwood, and pokeweed. But all in all, it was a great morning in this isolated wetland sheltering so many creatures.

June 6, 1994

Ah, Spring

Is it robins hopping on the lawn? Bees buzzing in crocus cups? Orchard buds blushing pink? Is it scales dropping from pussy-willows to reveal gray velvet? What tells you that winter's long sleep is over, that springtime is at hand. A gentler feeling in the air? The plaintive *peent* of a courting woodcock in a low meadow at dusk? More gold on weeping willows? A bluer tint to the sky?

Ever since the winter solstice, days started lengthening and small changes are occurring daily in our natural world. Skunk cabbages sent up tightly furled green leaf cones last September. Now that their strange internal furnaces are activated, dark red flower spathes are forcing up through ice and snow. (Air inside the spathe can be as much as fifty degrees warmer than outside air, so great is the heat the root generates.) Fetid odors of tiny blossoms on the spadix attract early gnats.

A few marsh-marigolds buds on the Nature Center's Beechwood Trail showed bright yellow February 18th, only to be put on hold a few days later with the season's heaviest snowfall and coldest temperatures.

Sap rises in trunks of all trees as their mighty internal pumps start again. We notice it especially in sugar maples whose sap we tap and distill. Large stands of these trees are dying in eastern Canada and New England, probably from acid rain, so midwestern trees become more important.

If you enjoy watching catkins develop, search out birches and alders which soon will be in blossom. Alders are interesting because they have last year's cones, this year's flowers, and next year's fruits all present at the same time. A stalk of their catkins brought in now will keep your windowsill in gold for a week.

Sighting the first spring butterfly, the mourning cloak, is always a joyous moment. It is perfectly camouflaged when resting on tree bark, but if its reddish brown wings open to reveal its bright yellow outside band, identification is certain.

In damp woodlands, red maples are blossoming. Ferns emerge, their new fronds heavily covered with furry hairs to protect them from cold. Soon, delicate fiddleheads will stretch up and start uncurling.

Sturdy deep-rooted dandelions, white chickweed, and purple henbit—familiar lawn and garden exotics—flower early, even when the ground is stiff with frost, so well-prepared are they for spring's return.

The robins are back from the south, lured by rising temperatures, frost retreating from the ground, and earthworms leaving hibernation. The worms wintered below frostline clustered in tight balls of 100 or more, their way of avoiding cold.

When pulling up to a country road stop sign, listen

for bird songs as welcome as a robin's caroling: the *see you see yeeer* of eastern meadowlarks and *conk la ree* of red-winged blackbirds, personifications of field and marsh.

Stunning blue belted kingfishers soon will rattle above rivers, one of the few avian species in which females have more color than males. Watch for her pretty rust belly band. In a quiet backwater, shivery-shaky masses of frog eggs are being laid.

American tree sparrows, purple finches, and dark-eyed juncos fly back north by early April. In their stead we'll find newly arrived friendly song, natty fox, and demure field sparrows. They are followed later by the handsome, sweet whistlers, white-throated and white-crowned sparrows. Geese and ducks also move north in huge flocks, spaced in V's or straggling lines high overhead.

At the edges of Nature Center paths, minute, easy-to-miss harbinger of spring is found in full blossom, often in a snowbank remnant. A brilliant scarlet cup mushroom is another early arrival, visible by March 12th last year.

If you know where spice-bush grows, keep watching for its tiny golden globes. And be ready for flashes of blue that mean eastern bluebirds and tree swallows are back. Who wants to live where there isn't a season called spring?

March 19, 1989

Popping Day

"Is it Popping Day yet?" I used to ask my mother as days went by with spring poised on the doorstep, but never making it all the way in. I'd counted crocus blossoms every day, an annual spring ritual. We'd had our usual debate: was seeing a flower had grown the same as seeing it grow. Pussy-willows were duly admired, but I was ready for magnolias to shed their velvet sepals and explode into blossoms, for dandelions to cover every field as if there were no tomorrow, for trees to dress their bare branches. I wanted jump ropes and marbles on the playground at school.

Finally, Popping Day came and still does, especially if we have a couple of warm twenty-four hour periods. The daffodil bed is aglow. Cherries and plums are cheery all over town. The vegetable garden is filled with flowering purple dead nettle and dainty little white chickweed flowers. Have you tried the game of watching for chickweed flowers to be in blossom every month of the year? It really does happen.

When popping out time finally comes, harbinger of spring, hepatica, and bloodroot have faded, but what a flood tide of wildflowers they usher in. What's your favorite? Golden marsh-marigolds? Pristine large flowered trillium? Acres of pink spring-beauty? Charming little blue-eyed Mary? Too many pretties to choose just one?

Low morning sun rays paint satiny beech trunks purpley silver and make its pointed coppery buds turn bright gold. At branch tips, the first leaves popping out have finely serrated edges protected from cold winds with infinitely fine down.

Birch trees have tiny heart-shaped leaves and dangling yellow-green catkins, graceful beyond human capacity to design. e. e. cummings wrote of "the leaping, greenly spirit of trees."

Horse-chestnut's sticky, dark red buds are popping flower and compound leaf structures of incredible complexity. What strength must be in their sap to support such a large and explosive volume of growth.

Most forest edges are a soft haze of harmonious pastel shades of red and green as buds expand and leaves emerge. Red maples have already flowered and adorned forest floors with masses of tiny scarlet and gold petalless flowers.

Norway maples popped overnight and are globes of pale yellow-green. As you pass, a buzz of dozens of busy bees is audible. Willows, whose branches have been unbelievably golden since January, wear a greenish cast as they flower and send out tiny new leaves.

Still-bare oaks finally dropped last year's leaves and soon will show tiny new ones and quantities of dangling catkin-like flower arrangements as days continue to lengthen.

Early nesting resident house finches are feeding their young while other birds carry nest-building materials. Tree swallows swoop back and forth over lakes, feeding on the wing. The usually raucous blue jay has assumed the quiet dignity that parenthood requires, but cardinals still whistle vigorously from tops of the tallest trees. An eastern bluebird has five azure eggs in her neatly woven grass bowl in the new nesting box.

Now we can be out of doors after supper. We hear the chant of a whip-poor-will and the *peent* of a nighthawk as he power dives above his mate.

Kinglets and yellow-rumped warblers flit through trees and a vagrant maple sprout pops out of last year's seed. My soul pops, too. It's spring again.

May 5, 1994

Midsummer Flowers

Bright orange daylilies and sky blue chicory flowers ornamenting roadsides tell us it's high summer. Queen Anne's lace is beginning to spread its lacy wares. In meadows, these floral displays are shoulder high, but at road's edge they are smaller and less vigorous.

An early morning walk in a dew-spangled meadow this time of year makes me feel as if I live on the Continent rather than in Michigan; nearly all the lovely summer field flowers are of European origin. Forked catchfly and hoary alyssum are busy setting seed, and it's a good time to gather common yarrow flowers for winter bouquets. Hang stems upside down in a sheltered place for a few days to let them dry thoroughly.

Oyster plant, also called goat's beard, is setting its large, beautifully round seed heads complete with golden-stemmed airy parachutes. Just think: this inconspicuous flower which opened for only a few hours transforms itself almost overnight into something unique and ethereal.

Ox-eye daisy, smoothly named *Chrysanthemum leucanthemum*, has faded, but its seed heads guarantee us future pleasures. So simple, the pure white and pure yellow blossom is designed with balanced and radial symmetry and is a favorite of many flower folk.

Alien clovers, pea family members, are everywhere: sturdy red clover spheres, prostrate little black medick with its tiny golden balls and twisted black seed pods, tall yellow sweet clover, and fuzzy heads and silky foliage of rabbit's foot clover. Low rays of the rising sun, shining through a large stand of grayish-pink rabbit's foot blossoms, create a delightfully soft and luminous rosy haze, sparkled here and there with dewdrop rainbows. Cow vetch is also an alien, but what lovely blue-purple masses its spikes make. Soon, downy little pea pods develop. Dainty curling tendrils at the end of every leaf are one of this flower's charms.

Milkweeds are a native family which add much beauty to summer fields and roadsides. Butterfly-weed has stunning orange blossoms contrasting pleasingly with lush blue-green foliage. It is a favorite with butterflies, as its name implies, and is a nature photographer's delight. Sand, or blunt-leaved, milkweed has finished blossoming and is busy growing a few pods. These plants have a complicated pollinating process and not many insects carry it off properly. Fortunately, many seeds in a pod compensate for small numbers of pods. Common milkweed's rosy globes are everywhere. Caterpillars are chomping away on leaves, and honeybees are busy at flowers. Swamp milkweed soon will show its deeper pink blossoms in wet areas, and some shady damp roadsides may have a white poke milkweed.

Venus' looking-glass, a native plant, appears here and there in sterile, sandy fields. Its tiny flowers are a pleasing shade of blue-violet. It also has cleistogamous, self-fertilizing blossoms which never open but produce fertile seeds guaranteed not to be cross-pollinated.

A walk in the Nature Center's prairie adds gray-headed coneflower, lead plant, prairie dock, bergamot, tall coreopsis, and delicate nodding Canada wild rye grass to your species list. Black-eyed Susan, too. Spiderwort shows its purple-stemmed stamens, bearing the loveliest fur of any flower I know. Use a magnifying glass to enjoy lush golden anthers atop royal purple fur. If you were designing flowers, what patterns could you design? What textures? What colors? What special charms?

Stroll a few minutes along the Kal-Haven Trail and you will find more native wildflowers along with thousands of common ragweed plants not yet in flower. Blossoming now or soon are woodland sunflower, prairie rosinweed, lion's foot, dogbane, and an inconspicuous enchanter's nightshade. Watch for wild yam, too.

Add some new friends to your list.

July 30, 1989

191

The Purple Time

In *Borland Country*, the author describes late summer and early fall as "the purple time." Indeed it is. Gone are the tender pastels of spring-beauty and hepatica, replaced through the summer by sky-blue roadside chicory and brilliant yellow-oranges of black-eyed Susan and butterfly-weed. As days grow shorter and the sun's rays longer, summer's accumulation of sunshine and heat brings a vivid harvest in masses of showy purple accented by bright goldenrods.

In roadside ditches, where no mowing has been done, dignified showy New England asters come into their own, often in glorious abundance. A tall, erect, well-branched flower, fond of moist meadows, it has lush foliage of dark green, lance-shaped, toothless leaves which clasp the sturdy stem with lobes that extend part way around it. From August to late October, these plants are graced with clusters of rich, soft but bright purple blossoms, a deeper violet than other asters. Pink forms are rarely found. Dense ray flowers may be three-quarters of an inch long and surround the central orange disk flowers. Such glowing luster.

Other common fall asters pale next to the wonders of the New England one, yet each adds its own touch of loveliness to the purple time. Watch especially for silky, azure, panicled, and purple-stemmed species. The Peterson and McKenney *Field Guide to Wildflowers, Northeastern* is especially helpful in sorting out field marks of lavender asters.

Aster is the Greek word for star. Truly, these members of the composite family are stars.

On dry wooded hills and in shady oak woods, colonies of the large-leaved aster cover many places. The foliage is often more striking than the meek pale violet blossoms because only a few plants flower. Leaves are thick, hairy, stalked, and heart-shaped and may be four to eight inches across. Large-leaved asters block out neighbors because toxic substances from their roots prevent other plants from growing.

In moist meadows and at trail edges, sturdy erect ironweed may grow nine feet tall, crowned with flattopped clusters of unrivaled reddish-purple brilliance. Of ironweed Borland wrote, "There is a purple to catch any eye, and hold it, a magnificent purple." When mixed with a field of goldenrod, ironweed is at its colorful best. Its many tiny flowers form a thistle-like head. The genus *Vernonia* honors an English botanist, William Vernon, who collected plants in North America. The common name comes from its coarse, hard stem which was thought to be iron hard by farmers trying to get rid of it.

Another purple flowering plant of rich moist soil and roadside ditches, and a certainty in late summer, is five-to six-foot tall spotted Joe Pye weed. Its magenta-red or pinky-purple heads are soft and fuzzy, eye-catching, set off by the white purity of boneset and snakeroot neighbors. Pye was a New England herbalist about whom various legends persist. Was he an Indian who helped Puritans in the early seventeenth century with his nostrums? Or did he buy rum in the Stockbridge tavern in July 1775 to increase his medicine's potency?

Purplish holdovers from summer may still be found: wild bergamot, blazing star, purple vetch, and pinky-purple globes of common milkweed.

If you're fortunate to be near a bit of true prairie, there may be a few of the long-lasting purple coneflowers still in blossom. This grand perennial has drooping purple petals on a two-inch wide orange centered flower.

Thistles and burdocks are purple, too. I have mixed feelings about burdock because I once saw a tiny ruby-throated hummingbird who couldn't get loose from the hooked barbs. They were stronger than the bird.

Keep watch for lavender and mauve blossoms in your roadsides and fields. Enjoy the purple time.

September 9, 1993

Signals of Change

Which autumn sounds, colors, tastes, or smells do you anticipate? Do you look forward to the cool, fresh atmosphere with its misty dawns and fields bright with wildflowers? Some are pleased by the arrival of hunting season or the sounds of sandhill cranes or Canada geese overhead. Others prefer the silken textures of thistledown or milkweed parachutes or scuffling through dry, fallen leaves.

Most of us enjoy the riot of color as changes occur in trees and shrubs creating a foliage fling. Do you look forward to the velvety smoky gold of tamaracks, or do you prefer watching dogwoods as they don multicolored coats? Sunshine through their tawny peach or rich deep scarlet is a delight.

Everyone has special memories of this season. When I was growing up, air pollution wasn't a concern. During weekends, suburbanites raked lawns and added that special blue haze and aroma of burning leaves to the atmosphere.

Sunny blueberry barrens develop a clear, ruddy glow as each tiny leaf stops manufacturing green chlorophyll and red pigments appear. A cool dry fall with lots of sunshine promotes the brilliant color. Sugars are made in the leaves during days while cool night temperatures clog their food and water tubes. The trapped sugar forms red pigment; frost kills this fleeting process. Area roadsides have many wild grape vines, notable for their yellow and golden shadings, pigments which were present all summer but masked by chlorophyll.

Do you ever wonder what causes leaves in deciduous forests to fall? It is abscission, an unseen process in which a small band of cells develops at the base of each leaf stalk. When these cells stop growing, the leaf falls. If you look closely at a twig where a leaf was fastened, you will see tiny dots where connecting tubes were closed, releasing the leaf from the stem. For reasons not fully understood, abscission cells do not develop in young beeches and some oaks until the following spring.

In woodlands, everything is changing. Where Virginia-creeper grew in sunshine, its leaves are gay as a paint box. On forest floors, look for bright scarlet nubbins of jack-in-the-pulpit seeds. Only yesterday they were shiny green kernels draped with a fading pulpit. Now pheasants and thrushes will dine on them.

As leaves drop, check your favorite trees to see what they've done to prepare for spring. Look for sticky, sharp golden buds on a cottonwood or tiny bright red orbs on a linden. Maple buds look ready to open.

When their leaves shrink, eye-catching purple-red stems of pokeweed appear. Long drooping fruit clusters change from green to dark blue or purple-black. Individual seeds, resembling tiny coins, are food for thrushes and catbirds. Historically, passenger pigeons ate thousands of them. Pigweeds turn red and become tumbleweeds. Fence rows may catch large numbers of these colorful globes.

Occasionally, a pasture or winter grain field is bright green whereas corn plants attain their usual soft, bleached appearance. Watch for an old-fashioned corn field interplanted with pumpkins.

Gay yellow witch hazel leaves often hide their blossoms of the same shade, our last flower of the year. After leaves drop, these flowers linger for many weeks brightening any autumn stroll.

September 25, 1988

Color Harvest

Autumn in southern Michigan steals in slowly with a scattering of red on sour gum trees and a migrating warbler or shorebird here and there. Sassafras often will drop one completely red mitten quite early. Autumn grasses are at their peak. This color spectacle and migration scene will continue for some weeks. Enjoy it.

September brings red berries on spice-bush. By October there will be incredibly delicate, rather oriental, wispy yellow flowers on witch hazel trees.

Colorful red maples thrive in low areas around lakes and creeks. Their red-orange-yellow spectrum against a brilliant blue cloudless sky can be breathtaking. Patches of vivid red shining sumac leaves, dramatic against still-green oaks, make me wish I could paint. Hike Kalamazoo Nature Center trails in fall to see a forest turned golden by great tulip trees on the Marsh Trail. Unforgettable. Or walk the boardwalk at West Lake Bog to see tamaracks turning gold.

A touch of frost or two will kill your tomato vines but it creates woodland palettes that thrill with an intensity and variety of color.

Chicory is lovely in late mornings along unmowed roadsides. Teale described it as the most beautiful blue under the sky, but I think fringed gentian gives chicory a hard race. If you live near a small lake, where someone hasn't grown a lawn right down to the edge, look there for gentians and shining white circlets of grass of Parnassus flowers.

The many yellow composites of autumn make ditches glow, a sight to store away in your mind and be retrieved on a gray, sleety December day.

If the birds haven't beaten you, stop for a tangy repast of fox-grapes. This plant, ancestor of Concord grapes, has large leathery leaves, so thick with pubescence that they're actually white underneath. River-bank grapes, found everywhere, are smaller. They make delicious juice and jelly but are pretty tart for eating from the vine.

Look for towering big bluestem at the Nature Center's reconstructed prairie. Little bluestem is notable for the delicacy of tiny, tiny starry seeds. These grasses with roots of up to twelve feet deep are remnants of tall grass prairies that once reached a long finger into Michigan. Imagine, if you can, hungry bison hordes feeding among thousands of acres of luxuriant grasses bowing gently to the prairie winds.

Hazel-nuts are ready to eat, but unfortunately squirrels learned that quite a while ago. While you're foraging for a forgotten nut, notice that next spring's catkins are already an inch long. Nature is such a good provider.

September 8, 1994

In Praise of Autumn

Radiant blue skies. Translucent tunnels on country lanes. Goose music floating down from on high. A drift of monarch butterflies. Migrant redstarts flitting in the bird bath. Crickets chirping relentlessly. Baseball bat-sized zucchinis lengthening in gardens. Apple tree branches bending to the ground laden with red fruit.

What tells you autumn has crept up on us again? What experiences do you cherish for October? Is it beds of chrysanthemums glowing like jewels? Is it the satisfactory sound of a shoe connecting squarely with a football? Perhaps it is pillows of mist resting lightly just above a tawny field that held amber waves of grain only days ago. Is it the sight of your neighbor crouched on hands and knees planting smooth brown bulbs?

For me, autumn is many things. Miniature Russian church tower buds on flowering dogwood trees. Grasses blowing gently. Rays of a low sun giving architectural grace to fields dotted with great rolls of hay. Orange pumpkins glowing in mountainous heaps at vegetable stands. White oaks turning wine color. Nursery schoolers pasting cutout leaves on windows. Grade schoolers using warm irons to preserve bright leaves between sheets of wax paper. I wonder: do college girls still wear big mums to football games?

In the woods, squirrels and chipmunks are busy hoarding beech and hickory nuts, acorns, fruit pits, evergreen cones, and tulip tree seeds in little caches. Last October, in walking some Comstock woods, we found three different sites where an animal had plucked one of the plentiful red *Russula* mushrooms and laid it in the branches of a shrub. No protection from weather or thievery, yet clearly an effort of harvesting and storage.

As sugar maple leaves magically turn luminous pale gold, a woodland walk is an experience in radiance. Leaves have drifted down one by one making a satisfying, crunching foot shuffle. Like a Persian carpet, the woodland floor is a palette of flame red, cranberry, russet, sepia, and copper.

At the edge of wetlands, orange and yellow jewelweeds are generously supplied with unique compressed seeds that explode in your hand when you pick them. Impatient they surely are. But what a special way to spread them far and wide and to satisfy our need for small wonderments.

Downy woodpeckers are busy harvesting mistletoe-like seeds from poison ivy vines. The seeds' fertility is not reduced by the bird's digestive system; therefore, he serves as a natural antidote to our earnest eradication efforts. Five to ten percent of his nourishment comes from berries of the *Rhus* family. Poison ivy's intense red fall color is its chief value for humans.

On a blue skies day, an ancient cottonwood, turned golden and sheathed in the scarlet of Virginia-creeper or poison ivy, is a likely subject to stimulate any artist.

Goldenrods, sunflowers, gentians, and asters, all flowers of field and prairie, come in many species and colors, adding much to the fairyland atmosphere of autumn landscapes. A bright expanse of old-field goldenrod, dotted with tawny bracken fern fronds and sun shot with scrubby scarlet staghorn sumacs, is a warming memory to recall on a snowy, sub-zero morning. In sandy areas, the small but beautifully shaped flax-leaved aster spreads a lavender carpet, adding a wash of soft pastel.

Michigan lakes reflect the charms of autumn skies. I remember a calendar of the colors of Lake Michigan hanging in The Art Institute of Chicago. The square for each October day was filled in with a different tint of blue, green, aqua, turquoise, gray, a telling description of the changing beauty of nature. 'Tis truly a season to celebrate, even as we sense farewell to yet another year.

Finally, the last little warbler has migrated, the last half songs of white-throated sparrows are silenced, the last ruby red leaf has fallen as autumn fades away. Robert Frost, in *After Apple Picking*, wrote: "Essence of winter sleep is on the night." In *In Memoriam*, Alfred, Lord Tennyson, wrote: "Calm and deep peace on this high wold." But perhaps the prophet Isaiah, who knew not the stirring glories of autumn colorings, phrased it best when he wrote so simply: "The whole world is at rest, and is quiet."

October 1, 1989

Winter Woodlands

After leaves have fallen, you discover many things hidden since spring. Characteristic shapes of trees, their trunk and branch arrangements, are now apparent for our pleasure and study.

Some scientists think you never have to look at the leaf of an oak tree to figure out its species; just study the tree's silhouette and the color and patterns of its bark. This takes lots of practice. Start with a pin oak and its drooping branches. Then, examine other trees. Red oak has a straight unbranched trunk with flat shiny planes. White oak bark has distinctive circular light target marks. The size and shape of acorns can be helpful if the critters have left any. Buds are in clusters of threes and fours at the end of branches.

Many oaks hold their leaves over winter, not dropping them until spring growth finally pushes them off. Beech trees, members of the oak family, also hold their bleached leaves among unique coppery-gold, furled, pointed buds all winter. Their gray bark, smooth even in maturity, is readily recognizable, a distinctive field mark.

In October, pussy willows had already pulled back their dark red bud scales exposing tips of gray velvet. I wonder if they'll be blighted by subfreezing temperatures.

Last year's sassafras twigs remain dark green, and their fat rounded cone buds are also green. Chewing a bit of aromatic twig will tell you for sure what it is. Basswood, or American linden, has tiny fat round buds, much smaller than those of sassafras; they are a surprising bright red.

Flowering dogwood's flower buds are unmistakable. In rugged climates, they blight from too many days of sub-zero cold or are eaten by rodents if deep snow cover is prolonged.

Locations of birds' nests always come as a surprise. Who would suspect that so many were close by? Birds were obvious all summer, but we were not aware of their home sites. Winter is a good time to learn locations of large woodland stick and leaf nests. Several of the hawks will return to the same nest a second year or will refurbish someone else's. Make a note of where to watch come spring.

Finding signs of birds in winter requires patience and a sharp eye. Check holes in trunks and large branches for screech owls or American kestrels. Ring-necked pheasants will feed on corn in your yard if the area hasn't been hunted out.

Looking at plants in winter is an interesting way to increase your botanical awareness. But beware. In summer "leaves of three, let it be" is a good warning for poison ivy, but what should you look for in winter? Long ago, before I was into nature, we chaperoned a student holiday weekend over New Year's. Walking dune moorlands, we found mistletoe and gaily tucked sprays of the white berries into hats or behind ears. Later, Student Health Clinic doctors were puzzled about the outbreak of scalp rashes and itching. It was years before I realized what we had done. So, watch for white berries. Oil, the irritant, causes some people trouble year-round. Also, look for vines with tendrils attached to trees by thousands of aerial rootlets. If you know where poison ivy grows in summer, study those plants. Note that the large leaf scars are half-round with sets of bundle scars. Once sure of its location, you can prowl around observing seeds and buds of other plants.

Small holes in the ground seem to appear suddenly when grass shrivels and forest floor light increases. Who lives in or made all these? Snakes? Little furry four-footed things? How can you tell a chipmunk's hole from a red squirrel's? One winter I found more than 200 jack pine cones, caches of red squirrels, tucked away near the bottom of a two cord heap of firewood. Along with them were several quarts of grass stems, all providently gathered and stored against deep snows. What endless fetching and carrying is involved in building a hoard of hundreds of cones. Don't other animals steal them? Is it a group pantry?

A red-headed woodpecker fills holes with acorns and other seeds, holes too deep for him or any other bird to get at. He puts bits of bark in place to seal the entrance.

Later, he carefully chisels out a new door, low down, and extracts the food.

When there's fresh snow, animal tracks give the woods walker a real challenge. One Christmas morning at Grand Canyon we went out early into newly fallen snow. All along the rim trail was a dainty track, clearly left by one of Santa's reindeer the previous night.

As an amateur at tracking I've never gotten much beyond the deer stage. I can't tell a raccoon's footprint from a skunk's or the single line of a fox from a pet dog. When we were doing a Christmas bird count north of Yellowknife in far northern Canada, hoping for a gyrfalcon, I was shown a bear print. That was pretty impressive. I'd still recognize one anywhere. When you're tracking, it's important to note length and width of tracks, distance apart, and number and arrangement of toes. Then find a good field guide.

December 18, 1990

Winter Thaw

Roaming a wintry woods during a prolonged thaw between storms is always fun, often instructive. Many leaves are matted from the weight of earlier snows but tough oak leaves still crunch under foot. Some from red oaks are enormous; they must be twelve inches from tip to tip. Red maple leaves, and a few from the grape vines that loop from tree top to tree top, have a strange mauve cast. Is this a fungus or just the way their natural fuzziness deteriorates? Sassafras and big-toothed aspen leaves are intact still, whereas black walnuts deteriorated leaving only their long stems.

Even though it's clearly winter, spring buds on some trees are evident. Plentiful numbers of red maple flower buds look ready to pop, pointed sassafras leaf buds are green, and dogwood buds are plump.

Erect little grape ferns look as perky and fresh as if it had never snowed, but long fronds of wood fern, still verdant, lie flat. Finely cut winter ferns have turned distinctive bronzy red. Ebony spleenwort's central fertile fronds are erect but its smaller sterile ones are flattened. Bleached fronds of bracken, in the dryest part of the woods, are completely flat as are those of sensitive ferns.

Wide expanses of club mosses are green as ever with a few spots of snow still shining white around some clusters. *Lycopodium* as a whole is a strange and unusual group, rare in many places. Tiny candelabra on the common form, ground pine, develop vast numbers of pollen grains that once provided flash powder for photography. Strange that deer don't seem to eat this lush and succulent plant, nor its cousin, the shining club moss.

Evidence of deer is everywhere, especially their wedge-shaped foot prints in recently thawed earth. Along the marsh edge there are clear places pawed in the ground where a rutting stag left his territorial marks. In one place, he broke off several blue-green curled horns of an emerging skunk cabbage.

A large rock by an old hackberry tree serves as a breakfast nook for resident squirrels and there lies their litter--remains of hundreds and hundreds of black walnuts. Multiple tooth marks are clearly visible on both sides of every nutshell. How tiresome to have to work so hard to get one's nourishment. Try biting one yourself.

Mosses and lichens around tree trunk bases are bright green, although only a week ago they were totally buried in snow. Their ways of surviving in winter are remarkable.

Where the little creek met obstacles, splashed water froze sheathing red osier-dogwood and pasture rose stems with ice and many tiny icicle dribbles. Iced rose hips are sparkling jewels.

Several times along the path I found large splinters

of wood, fresh and new. A pileated woodpecker must have been exploring dead trunks for his favorite ant colonies and left his telltale evidence behind.

February 11, 1995

A Snowy Day

I walked a fresh and snowy woods today. Every twig, every bud, every wizened apple, every blade of grass, every aster seed star flaunted frostings of white-as-white fluff. The absence of any breezes meant that each little decorative pouf on Queen Anne's intricate laces remained in place, turning the woodland into a wonderland. With no wind and no sun, there were no drifts and no icicles, just a transforming coat of white on every single surface.

Effulgence is not a common word, but it best describes the glow and purity of the amazing whiteness everywhere. Although snow flakes were still gently wandering down, leaden clouds in the southern sky thinned momentarily. Evanescent bits of softly veiled blue and a shining spot appeared where the winter sun's radiance peered through.

Because the thermometer read thirty-three degrees, single sparkling crystals were not apparent as they would be on a bone-chilling day when your mind is boggled by myriad crystalline shapes. Old ice on the little pond was soft and mushy. New flakes melted on contact.

Each scarlet multiflora rose hip had its leaning nightcap as soft snowy buildups tipped slightly. Domes on European mountain-ash berry clusters looked like meringue on a pie, so thick and luscious were they.

Each flared vaselike seed urn that paraded up an evening primrose stalk had a chic spotless chapeau. Hawthorns' long spikes helped hold the damp, heavy snow in place, filling branches with solid masses of whiteness punctuated only by dark reddish-brown thorn lines.

In the whitened landscape, evergreen trees had snow icing where clustered needles created receptacles. More snow, wind, even rain and sleet, could not reach the trees' trunks due to the dense outer blankets. Here birds take shelter from the bitterness.

The woodland was so beautiful in its total whiteout that I almost forgot my intended purpose of studying tree forms, a project easiest in winter. Beeches are unmistakable with their grayed-mauve bark, lustrous coppery cigar shaped buds, and bleached leaves.

Long-stemmed seed balls and multicolored peeling bark identify sycamores. The tall, ever-so-straight, unbranched trunks with upright seed cones are tulip trees. Dangling catkins decorate hazel-nut bushes and clusters of canoe paddle seeds hang from box elders. Leaf buds on flowering dogwoods are tiny and pointed. Hackberry bark is rough with irregular shallow ridges.

Barometric pressure has dropped slowly since early morning. Birds, sensitive to this storm warning, remain in hiding. Because wet feathers limit birds' aeronautical efficiency, they will perforce eat lightly today. A lone, silent crow wings his way across lowering skies.

A band of American goldfinches would usually be dancing from birch to birch feeding on dangling columns of miniature seeds and sending quantities of trefoil shaped bracts a-flying. Today the woods were silent, not even a chattering chickadee.

Cottontail rabbits, out of their cupped dry grass beds early, left telltale autographs in the fresh snow as they hunted winter fare of buds and twigs. Isn't it fun that prints of their hind feet are ahead of the front? A neighbor's dog left his strangely straight line of tracks.

In one bare spot under a leaf-bearing oak, sharp pale green points of daffodil leaves were visible. An encouraging sign, even if I know their flowering is weeks away. What a day to discover and study magical and charming new forms and patterns nature created with this pure blanket of water, metamorphosed into a fluffy ever-so-white cover.

January 21, 1995

To Study a Season

Walking in a wetland in winter is first-rate fun. Footing may be uncertain depending on how cold it's been, but that's part of the pleasure. Just choose a marsh or swamp where water isn't too deep. Better wear good boots and take a walking stick. Then you won't grab the nearest poison sumac for an anchor.

With no leaves on trees and shrubs, and no insects to plague you if you stop to look at something, the curious can find many interesting things to observe.

One of the first things to catch your eye will be bleached cattail stalks waving lazily. Furry spikes are frowzy-blowzy by now. Take time to investigate the satin soft fuzz to find a tiny seed. A hand lens may help you. Remember, scientists say there are a million seeds in every spike.

The wintry landscape is a monotone of tan and brown making bright red stems of red osier-dogwood and the vibrant green sphagnum moss mounds welcome contrasts. In open water you'll see that watercress and duckweed stay green all twelve months despite endless freezing and thawing.

Most fruit stems on gray dogwood have dropped by now, but any remaining delicate skeletons are bright maroon. On higher clear spots, leaves of motherwort and golden ragwort are brilliant green all winter.

A few clusters of ivory beads, shiny as billiard balls, droop from poison sumac branches. Bright red berries cling to high-bush cranberry, winterberry, Japanese barberry, and multiflora rose, good reasons to stick around if you're a robin or a hermit thrush.

Close inspection of tamarack branches reveals a few, tiny perfectly formed cones. Maturing in their first season, cones persist on the tree for a year or more. This proves that tamaracks really are conifers despite their annual needle drop. A few remaining needles are bleached to soft gold, lustrous in the slanting sun's rays.

Sensitive ferns turned tawny brown on the first night near thirty-two degrees, hence their name. Their unusual spore stalks hold little strings of tiny round brown beads sturdily erect. You'll find that some dry pinnules have split to release spores; others are still hard, solid balls.

On red maple twigs, look for the most recent year's growth which will be red, a contrast to older gray bark.

Pitcher-plant leaves are deep bright red, the same shade as their June flower petals. Is this because photosynthesis doesn't occur in winter? Their silvery hairs, which prevent insects' escape, contrast vividly.

Marsh grasses are worth special study this time of year. Most brown seeds of tall, graceful Indian grass have dropped; clinging hulls are transparent, holding sparkling dew or frost in the interstices. Tiny seed cups on bog arrow grass stalks demonstrate the grace of repetition.

Stately great water-dock's sturdy stems, four to six feet tall, hold many of their intriguing three-angled seeds, marvels of design. Finely fluted stalks are as elegant as any Parthenon column.

Watch for swamp aster's starry sepals and fuzzy goldenrod heads, seemingly designed to trap fleecy snowflakes.

January 9, 1992

Common and Scientific Names
Alien species are marked with an *

A

Alder, *Alnus* spp.
*Alyssum, hoary, *Berteroa incana*
Anemone, Canada, *Anemone canadensis*
Arbor vitae. *See* Cedar, northern white
Arbutus, trailing, *Epigaea repens*
Arrowhead, *Sagittaria latifolia*
Ash
  black, *Fraxinus nigra*
  prickly, *Zanthoxylum americanum*
  white, *Fraxinus americana*
Ash-leaved maple. *See* Box elder
Aspen
  big-toothed, *Populus grandidentata*
  quaking, *Populus tremuloides*
Aster
  azure. *See* sky-blue
  bristly, *Aster puniceus*
  flax-leaved. *See* stiff
  large-leaved, *Aster macrophyllus*
  New England, *Aster novae-angliae*
  panicled, *Aster lanceolatus* var. *simplex*

Blue-eyed Mary, *Collinsia verna*
Blue-hearts, *Buchnera americana*
Bobwhite, northern, *Colinus virginianus*
Bog-rosemary, *Andromeda glaucophylla*
Boneset, *Eupatorium perfoliatum*
Box elder, *Acer negundo*
Bumblebee, family Apidae
Bunting
  indigo, *Passerina cyanea*
  snow, *Plectrophenax nivalis*
*Burdock, *Arctium minus*
Butterfly-weed, *Asclepias tuberosa*
Butternut, *Juglans cinerea*
Buttonbush, *Cephalanthus occidentalis*

C

Cardinal-flower, *Lobelia cardinalis*
Cardinal, northern, *Cardinalis cardinalis*
Catalpa, *Catalpa bignoniodes*
Catbird, gray, *Dumetella carolinensis*
Catbrier. *See* Greenbrier, common
*Catchfly, forked, *Silene dichotoma*
Cattail
  broad-leaved. *See* common
  common, *Typha latifolia*
  narrow-leaved, *Typha angustifolia*
Cedar
  red. *See* red, eastern
  red, eastern, *Juniperus virginiana*
  white, northern, *Thuja occidentalis*

Common and Scientific Names

Cherry, black, *Prunus serotina*
Chickadee
  black-capped, *Parus atricapillus*
  boreal, *Parus hudsonicus*
Chickweed, *Stellaria media*
Chicory, *Cichorium intybus*
Cinquefoil, shrubby, *Potentilla fruticosa*
Clover
  *rabbit foot, *Trifolium arvense*
  *red, *Trifolium pratense*
Colic-root, *Aletris farinosa*
Columbo, American, *Frasera caroliniensis*
Compass-plant, *Silphium laciniatum*
Coneflower
  gray-headed, *Ratibida pinnata*
  purple, *Echinacea purpurea*
Coreopsis, tall, *Coreopsis tripteris*
Cormorant, double-crested, *Phalacrocorax auritus*
Cotton-grass, *Eriophorum* spp.
Cottonwood, eastern, *Populus deltoides*
Cowbird, brown-headed, *Molothrus ater*
Cranberry, *Vaccinium* spp.
  high-bush, *Viburnum trilobum*
Crane, sandhill, *Grus canadensis*
Crossbill, white-winged, *Loxia leucoptera*
Crow
  American, *Corvus brachyrhynchos*
  fish, *Corvus ossifragus*
  northwestern, *Corvus caurinus*
Crowberry, *Empetrum* spp.

Cuckoo, yellow-billed, *Coccyzus americanus*
Cucumber, wild, *Echinocystis lobata*
Curlew, long-billed, *Numenius americanus*

D

*Daisy, ox-eye, *Chrysanthemum leucanthemum*
*Dandelion, *Taraxacum officinale*
*Day-lily, *Hemerocallis fulva*
Dead nettle, purple, *Lamium purpureum*
Dock, prairie, *Silphium terebinthinaceum*
Dogbane, spreading, *Apocynum androsaemifolium*
Dogberry, *Ribes cynosbati*
Dogwood
  flowering, *Cornus florida*
  gray, *Cornus racemosa*
  red osier, -*Cornus stolonifera*
Dove
  mourning, *Zenaida macroupa*
  rock, *Columba livia*
Duckweed, *Lemna* spp.
Duck, wood, *Aix sponsa*

E

Eagle, bald, *Haliaeetus leucocephalus*
Elm, American, *Ulmus americanus*
Evening-primrose, common, *Oenothera biennis*

F

Falcon, peregrine, *Falco peregrinus*

Common and Scientific Names

Fern
  bracken, *Pteridium aquilinum*
  chain, *Woodwardia virginica*
  Christmas, *Polystichum acrostichoides*
  cinnamon, *Osmunda cinnamomea*
  ebony spleenwort, *Asplenium platyneuron*
  grape, *Botrychium dissectum*
  marsh, *Thelypteris palustris*
  royal, *Osmunda regalis*
  sensitive, *Onoclea sensibilis*
  wood, *Dryopteris thelypteris*
Finch
  house, *Carpodacus mexicanus*
  purple, *Carpodacus purpureus*
Fir, Douglas, *Pseudotsuga taxifolia*
Flicker, northern, *Colaptes auratus*
Flycatcher
  great crested, *Myiarchus crinitus*
  vermillion, *Pyrocephalus rubinus*

G

*Garlic-mustard, *Alliaria petiolata*
Gentian
  centaury, showy, *Centarum pulchellum*
    closed, *Gentiana andrewsii*
  downy, *Gentiana puberula*
  fringed, *Gentiana crinita*
  lesser fringed, *Gentiana procera*
  rose-pink, *Sabatia angularis*
  soapwort, *Gentiana saponaria*

Common and Scientific Names

Grass (*cont.*)
  Indian, *Sorghastrum nutans*
  Junegrass, *Koeleria pyrimidata*
  marram. *See* beach-
  prairie
    cord, *Spartina pectinata*
    rye, Canada wild, *Elymus canadensis*
Grass of Parnassus, *Parnassia glauca*
Grebe, pied-billed, *Podilymbus podiceps*
Greenbrier, common, *Smilax rotundifolia*
Grosbeak
  evening, *Coccothraustes vespertinus*
  pine, *Pinicola enucleator*
  rose-breasted, *Pheucticus ludovicianus*
Grouse
  ruffed, *Bonasa umbellus*
  sharp-tailed, *Tympanuchus phasianellus*
  spruce, *Dendragapus canadensis*
Gyrfalcon, *Falco rusticolus*

H

Hackberry, northern, *Celtis occidentalis*
Harbinger of spring, *Erigenia bulbosa*
Hardhack, *Spiraea tomentosa*
Hawk
  red-tailed, *Buteo jamaicensis*
  rough-legged, *Buteo lagopus*
Hawthorn
  downy, *Crataegus mollis*
  *English, *Crataegus monogyna*

Washington, *Crataegus phaeropyrum*
Hazel-nut, American, *Corylus americana*
Heath family, Ericaceae
Hemlock, eastern, *Tsuga canadensis*
*Henbit, *Lamium amplexicaule*
Hepatica, *Hepatica* spp.
Heron, great blue, *Ardea herodias*
Hickory, *Carya* spp.
Holly, Michigan. *See* Winterberry
*Horse-chestnut, *Aesculus hippocastanum*
Horsetail, *Equisetum* spp.
Hummingbird, ruby-throated, *Archilochus colubris*

I

Impatiens. *See* Jewel-weed
Indigo, white false, *Baptisia bracteata*
Inkberry. *See* Pokeweed
Iris
  blue
    northern, *Iris versicolor*
    southern, *Iris virginica*
    *yellow, *Iris pseudacorus*
Ironweed, *Vernonia fasciculata*
Ivy, poison, *Toxicodendron radicans*

J

Jack-in-the-pulpit, *Arisaema triphyllum*
Jaeger, long-tailed, *Stercorarius longicaudus*
Jay
  blue, *Cyanocitta cristata*

Jay (*cont.*)
  gray, *Perisoreus canadensis*
  Steller's, *Cyanocitta stelleri*
Jewel-weed, *Impatiens capensis*
Joe Pye weed, spotted, *Eupatorium maculatum*
Junco, dark-eyed, *Junco hyemalis*
Juneberry. *See* Serviceberry
Juniper, *Juniperus* spp.

K

Killdeer, *Charadrius vociferus*
Kingbird, eastern, *Tyrannus tyrannus*
Kingfisher, belted, *Ceryle alcyon*
Kinglet, *Regulus* spp.

L

Lark, horned, *Eremophila alpestris*
Laurel, swamp, *Kalmia polifolia*
Lead-plant, *Amorpha canescens*
Leatherleaf, *Chamaedaphne calyculata*
Lichen, group Lichenes
  reindeer, *Cladonia* spp.
Lily, Michigan, *Lilium michiganense*
Linden, American. *See* Basswood
Lion's foot. *See* Rattlesnake-root
Lizard's tail, *Saururus cernuus*
Lobelia, great blue, *Lobelia siphilitica*
Loon, *Gavia* spp.

M

Magnolia, *Magnolia grandiflora*
Magpie, *Pica* spp.
Mallard, *Anas platyrhyncos*
Maple
  *Norway, *Acer platanoides*
  red, *Acer rubrum*
  silver, *Acer saccharum*
  sugar, *Acer saccharinum*
Marsh-marigold, *Caltha palustris*
Mayflower. *See* Arbutus, trailing
May tree. *See* Hawthorn, English
Meadowlark, eastern, *Sturnella magna*
*Medick, black, *Medicago lupulina*
Milkweed
  common, *Asclepias syriaca*
  sand, *Asclepias amplexicaulis*
  swamp, *Asclepias incarnata*
Monarch, *Danaus plexippus*
Moorhen, *Gallinule chloropus*
Moss
  club, *Lycopodium* spp.
    groundpine, *Lycopodium obscurum*
    shining, *Lycopodium lucidulum*
  sphagnum, *Sphagnum* spp.
Moth, luna, *Actias luna*
*Motherwort, *Leonurus cardiaca*
Mountain-ash, European, *Sorbus acuparia*
Mourning cloak, *Nymphalis antiopa*
*Mulberry, white, *Morus alba*

Common and Scientific Names

*Mullein, common, *Verbascum thapsis*
*Myrtle, *Vinca minor*

N

Nettle, stinging, *Laportea canadensis*
Nighthawk, common, *Chordeiles minor*
Nightshade
  deadly, *Solanum dulcamara*
  enchanter's, *Circaea lutetiana*
Nutcracker, Clark's, *Nucifraga columbiana*
Nuthatch
  red-breasted, *Sitta canadensis*
  white-breasted, *Sitta carolinensis*

O

Oak
  black, *Quercus velutina*
  northern red, *Quercus rubra*
  pin, *Quercus palustris*
  white, *Quercus alba*
*Olive, autumn, *Elaeagnus umbellata*
Orchid
  dragon's mouth, *Arethusa bulbosa*
  fen orchis. *See* twayblade, Loesel's
  grass-pink, *Calopogon pulchellus*
  lady-slipper
    moccasin-flower. *See* lady-slipper, pink
    pink, *Cypripedium acaule*
    showy, *Cypripedium reginae*

Common and Scientific Names

Pine
  jack, *Pinus banksiana*
  white, *Pinus strobus*
Pipit, *Anthus* spp.
Pipsissewa. *See* Prince's pine
Pitcher-plant, *Sarracenia purpurea*
Plover, black-bellied, *Pluvialis squatarola*
Pokeweed, *Phytolacca americana*
*Poplar
  Carolina. *See* Cottonwood, eastern
    necklace. *See* Cottonwood, eastern
    silver, *Populus alba*
Prairie chicken, *Tympanuchus* spp.
Prairie smoke, *Geum triflorum*
Prickly pear, *Opuntia humifusa*
Prince's pine, *Chimaphila umbellata*
Ptarmigan, willow, *Lagopus lagopus*
Pussytoes, *Antennaria* spp.
Pyracantha, *Rosa* spp.

Q

*Queen Anne's lace, *Daucus carota*

R

Ragweed
  common, *Ambrosia artemisiifolia*
  giant, *Ambrosia trifida*
Ragwort, golden, *Senecio aureus*
Rail, Family Rallidae

black, *Lateralius jamaicensis*
Rattlesnake root, *Prenanthes alba*
Raven, common, *Corvus corax*
Redhaw. *See* Hawthorn, downy
Redpoll
  common, *Carduelis flammea*
  hoary, *Carduelis hornemanni*
Redstart, *Setophaga ruticilla*
Robin, American, *Turdus migratorius*
Rose
  *multiflora, *Rosa multiflora*
  pasture, *Rosa carolina*
Rosin-weed, prairie, *Silphium integrifolium*
Rush, Baltic, *Juncus balticus*

S

Sapsucker, yellow-bellied, *Sphyrapicus varius*
Sarvisberry. *See* Serviceberry
Sassafras, *Sassafras albidum*
Scarlet cup, *Sarcoscypha coccinea*
Scoter, white-winged, *Melanitta fusca*
Screwstem, *Bartonia virginica*
Seaside-spurge, *Euphorbia polygonifolia*
Serviceberry, *Amelanchier* spp.
Shadblow. *See* Serviceberry
Shadbush. *See* Serviceberry
Siskin, pine, *Carduelis pinus*
Skunk cabbage, *Symplocarpus foetidus*
Snakeroot, *Sanicula* spp.
Sour gum, *Nyssa sylvatica*

Common and Scientific Names

Sparrow
  American tree, *Spizella arborea*
  field, *Spizella pusilla*
  fox, *Passerella iliaca*
  house, *Passer domesticus*
  song, *Melospiza melodia*
Sparrow (*cont.*)
  white-crowned, *Zonotrichia leucophrys*
  white-throated, *Zonotrichia albicollis*
Spice-bush, *Lindera benzoin*
Spider
  burrowing, *Lycosa wrightii*
  orb, *Argiope* spp.
Spiderwort, smooth, *Tradescantia ohiensis*
Spring-beauty, *Claytonia virginica*
Spruce
  black, *Picea mariana*
  Sitka, *Picea sitchensis*
*Starling, European, *Sturnus vulgaris*
Steeplebush. *See* Hardhack
Stilt, black-necked, *Himantopus mexicanus*
Sumac
  poison, *Toxicodendron vernix*
  staghorn, *Rhus typhina*
Sundew, *Drosera* spp.
Sunflower, woodland, *Helianthus divaricatus*
Swallow
  bank, *Riparia riparia*
  barn, *Hirundo rustica*

tree, *Tachycineta bicolor*
Swallowtail
  giant, *Papilio crisphontes*
  spicebush, *Papilio troilus*
  zebra, *Eurytides marcellus*
Swan, tundra, *Cygnus columbianus*
Swertia. See Columbo, American
Sycamore, *Platanus occidentalis*

T

Tamarack, *Larix laricina*
Tanager, scarlet, *Piranga olivacea*
Teaberry. *See* Wintergreen
Tearthumb, halberd-leaved, *Polygonum arifolium*
Tern
  arctic, *Sterna paradisaea*
  black, *Childonias niger*
Thistle
  *bull-, *Cirsium vulgare*
Thorn apple tree. *See* Hawthorn
Thrasher, *Toxostoma* spp.
Thrush
  hermit, *Catharus guttatus*
  Swainson's, *Catharus ustulatus*
  wood, *Hylocichla mustelina*
Titmouse, tufted, *Parus bicolor*
Touch-me-not. *See* Jewel-weed
Trillium, big white, *Trillium grandiflorum*

Common and Scientific Names

Tulip tree, *Liriodendron tulipifera*
Turkey, wild, *Meleagris gallopavo*
Turtle
  map, *Graptemys geographica*
  painted, *Chrysemys picta*
Turtlehead, *Chelone glabra*
Twinflower, *Linnea borealis*

V

Veery, *Catharus fuscescens*
Venus' looking-glass, *Triodanis perfoliata*
Vetch
  *cow, *Vicia cracca*
  *purple, *Vicia villosa*
Violet
  bird-foot, *Viola pedata*
Vireo
  warbling, *Vireo gilvus*
  yellow-throated, *Vireo flavifrons*
Virginia-creeper, *Parthenocissus quinquefolia*

W

Walnut, black, *Juglans nigra*
Warbler
  blue-winged, *Vermivora pinus*
  Canada, *Wilsonia canadensis*
  Cape May, *Dendroica tigrina*
  hooded, *Wilsonia citrina*
  Kirtland's, *Dendroica kirtlandii*

magnolia, *Dendroica magnolia*
prothonotary, *Protonotaria citrea*
Wilson's, *Wilsonia pusilla*
yellow, *Dendroica petechia*
yellow-rumped, *Dendroica coronata*
  See also Yellowthroat, common
*Watercress, *Rorippa nasturtium-aquaticum*
Water-dock, great, *Rumex orbiculatus*
Water-lily
  sweet-scented, *Nymphaea odorata*
  yellow spatterdock, *Nuphar advena*
Water-plantain, *Alisma subcordatum*
Waxwing
  Bohemian, *Bombycilla garrulus*
  cedar, *Bombycilla cedrorum*
Whip-poor-will, *Caprimulgus vociferus*
Willow
  black, *Salix nigra*
  pussy-, *Salix discolor*
  sandbar-, *Salix exigua*
  *weeping, *Salix babylonica*
Wingstem, *Verbesina alternifolia*
Winterberry, *Ilex verticillata*
Wintergreen, *Gaultheria procumbens*
Wintergreen, spotted, *Chimaphila maculata*
Witch hazel, *Hamamelis virginiana*
  vernal, *Hamamelis vernalis*
Woodcock, American, *Scolopax minor*
Woodpecker
  acorn, *Melanerpes formicivorus*

Common and Scientific Names

Woodpecker (*cont.*)
  downy, *Picoides pubescens*
  hairy, *Picoides villosus*
  pileated, *Dryocopus pileatus*
  red-bellied, *Melanerpes carolinus*
  red-headed, *Melanerpes erythrocephalus*
  See also Flicker, northern
Wood-pewee, eastern, *Contopus virens*
Wren
  house, *Troglodytes aedon*
  marsh, *Cistothorus palustris*

Y

*Yarrow, common, *Achillea millefolium*
Yellowthroat, common, *Geothlypis trichas*
Yew, *Taxus canadensis*

Selective Bibiography

Barnes, Burton V. and Warren H. Wagner, Jr. *Michigan Trees: A Guide to the Trees of Michigan and the Great Lakes Region.* Ann Arbor, Michigan: The University of Michigan Press, 1981. (Originally published in 1913 as *Michigan Trees: A Handbook of the Native and Most Important Introduced Species* by Charles Herbert Otis.)

Borland, Hal G. *Borland Country*, Philadelphia: J. B. Lippincott Co., 1947.

——, *Countryman: A Summary of Belief.* Philadelphia: J. B. Lippincott Co., 1965.

Brewer, Richard. *The Science of Ecology.* Second Ed. New York: Saunders-Harcourt Brace, 1994.

——, Gail A. McPeek, and Raymond J. Adams, Jr. *The Atlas of Breeding Birds of Michigan.* East Lansing, Michigan: Michigan State University Press, 1991.

Brock, Kenneth J. *Birds of the Indiana Dunes.* Bloomington, Indiana: Indiana University Press, 1986.

Case, Fred. *Orchids of the Western Great Lakes Region.* Bulletin 48. Bloomfield Hills, Michigan: Cranbrook Institute of Science, 1987.

Comstock, Anna Botsford. *Handbook of Nature Study.* Ithaca, N. Y.: Comstock Publishing Co., 1911.

Eastman, John. *The Book of Forest and Thicket*. Mechanicsburg, Pennsylvania: Stackpole Books, 1995.

———. *The Book of Swamp and Bog*. Mechanicsburg, Pennsylvania: Stackpole Books, 1995.

Eckert, Allan W. *The Owls of North America*. Garden City, N. Y.: Doubleday & Co., 1974.

Forbush, Edward Howe. *Birds of Massachusetts and Other New England States, Part III*. Norwood, Massachusetts: Norwood Press, 1929.

Granlund, James, Gail A. McPeek, and Raymond J. Adams, Jr. *The Birds of Michigan*. Bloomington, Indiana: Indiana University Press, 1994.

Hanes, Clarence R. and Florence N. Hanes. *Flora of Kalamazoo County, Michigan*. Schoolcraft, Michigan, 1947.

Harrison, Hal H. *A Field Guide to Birds' Nests in the United States East of the Mississippi River*. Boston: Houghton Mifflin, 1975.

Homoya, Michael A. *Orchids of Indiana*. Published by the Indiana Academy of Science. Distributed by Indiana University Press. Bloomington and Indianapolis, Indiana, 1993.

Huggler, Tom. "What Good is a Prairie?" *Michigan Natural Resources Magazine*. March-April, 1988: 16-23.

Lampe, Kenneth F. and Mary Ann McCann. *American Medical Association Handbook of Poisonous and Injurious Plants*. Chicago: American Medical Association, 1985.

Madson, John. *Where the Sky Began: Land of the Tallgrass Prairie*. Boston: Houghton Mifflin, 1983.

Ogburn, Charlton. *The Adventure of Birds*. New York: Morrow Quill Paperbacks, 1975.

Otis, Charles. See Barnes, Burton V. and Warren H. Wagner, Jr.

Parker, Bertha Morris. *The Golden Treasury of Natural History*. New York: Simon and Schuster, 1952.

Peterson, Roger Tory and the Editors of *Life*. *The Birds*. New York: Time, 1963.
—— and Margaret McKenny. *A Field Guide to Wildflowers of Northeastern and Northcentral North America*. Boston: Houghton Mifflin, 1968.

Pippen, Richard W. "Biodiversity and Habitats." *State of the Kalamazoo County Environment*. Pp 31-42. Lansing, Michigan: House of Representatives, 1992.

Poole, Lynn and Gary Poole. *Insect-Eating Plants*. New York: T. Y. Crowell Co., 1963.

Rogers, Julia. *Trees Every Child Should Know*. New York: Grosset and Dunlap, 1909.

Rogers, Walter E. *Tree Flowers of Forest, Park and Street*. New York: Dover, 1965.

Sargent, Charles. *Manual of the Trees of North America*. New York: Dover, 1949, 1961.

Smith, Helen V. *Winter Wildflowers*. Ann Arbor, Michigan: The Michigan Botanical Club, 1973.

Swink, Floyd and Gerould Wilhelm. *Plants of the Chicago Region*. 4th Ed. Lisle, Illinois: The Morton Arboretum; Indianapolis: Indiana Academy of Sciences, 1994.

Teale, Edwin Way. *A Naturalist Buys an Old Farm*. New York: Ballantine Books, 1974.

Terborgh, John. *Where Have all the Birds Gone? Essays on the Biology and Conservation of Birds That Migrate to the American Tropics*. Princeton, N. J.: Princeton University Press, 1989.

Terres, John K. *The Audubon Society Encyclopedia of North American Birds*. New York: Alfred A. Knopf, 1980.

Voss, Edward G. *Michigan Flora: A Guide to the Identification and Occurrence of the Native and Naturalized Seed-Plants of the State*. Vol. I, 1972. Vol II, 1985. Bloomfield Hills, Michigan: Cranbrook Institute of Science.

Wallace, David Rains. *Life in the Balance*. Companion to the Audubon Television Specials. New York: Harcourt Brace Jovanovich, 1987.

Index

Index

Index

Index

About the Author

Emma Bickham Pitcher's serious nature interest started in the early 1950s in the Indiana Dunes where she began bird and flower watching. Moving there in 1980 from Chicago, she wrote and taught about dunes natural features, enjoying photography and field work. Since 1987, she has devoted many hours to the Kalamazoo Nature Center: studying the trails, teaching, and writing. A naturalist at a 180-acre private nature preserve and a licensed bird bander, she took courses at Michigan State University and Western Michigan University.

An Illinois native, Pitcher raised a family and then worked at the University of Chicago. At retirement, she was Dean of Students of the Graduate School of Business. Her writings include *Up and Down the Dunes* and articles in midwestern Audubon publications. Over the years, various awards in recognition of her volunteer activities have come her way, including those from the Michigan Audubon Society, the National Park Service, and the State of Indiana Order of the Sagamores of the Wabash.

Cover photo by the author.